COSIMO TURA

TURA

PAINTINGS AND DRAWINGS

COMPLETE EDITION

BY EBERHARD RUHMER

PHAIDON PUBLISHERS INC

DISTRIBUTED BY GARDEN CITY BOOKS
NEW YORK

MADE IN GREAT BRITAIN

TEXT PRINTED AT THE CURWEN PRESS · PLAISTOW · E.13

PLATES PRINTED BY GEO. GIBBONS · LEICESTER

BOUND AT THE PITMAN PRESS · BATH

LAY-OUT OF THE PLATES BY LUDWIG GOLDSCHEIDER · LONDON

FOREWORD

Interest in the art of Cosimo Tura has been steadily increasing since the beginning of the eighteenth century. A vast amount of material has been collected, but no general picture of the artist has been formed and the number of real Tura monographs is surprisingly small. An independent presentation of his life and work thus seemed all the more necessary, since this gives us the possibility of throwing more light on individual problems.

The chief task was the establishment of a reasonably accurate chronology of Tura's works. Starting from the few certain dates, the works have been divided into a number of groups. The chronological order thus achieved is of necessity a reconstruction, but at least it can lay claim to being 'natural' and logical. The Catalogue comprises all works by Tura that have been preserved, together with the lost works as to the existence of which we have certain evidence. To make the trend of development clearer, the Catalogue has been arranged chronologically, whether the works in question have been preserved or not and without regard to their location or nature.

The accomplishment of this task has resulted on the one hand in a diminution of Tura's hitherto recognized œuvre, and on the other hand in an enrichment of it. What did not fit in with the scheme of development had to be sacrificed, but existing gaps could be bridged by the inclusion of a certain amount of new material, which the chronological method showed to belong to Tura. Of prime importance in this connection are the frescoes in Palazzo Schifanoia, which have been restored to Tura's œuvre and find their natural place under the known date of their execution.

Scattered portions of composite pictures had, for urgent reasons, to be rearranged. This was particularly the case with the so-called Belfiore Allegories, the so-called San Luca altar-piece and a few other altar-pieces. Here more attention has been paid to perhaps excessively meticulous distinctions than to possibly wrong groupings.

The existing photographic material has to a large extent been replaced by new photographs, since most of Tura's works in recent times have been more or less completely restored, and also because there was a lack of good detail photos.

ACKNOWLEDGEMENTS

Our thanks are due in the first place to the founder and chief representative of modern study of Tura's art, Adolfo Venturi, and to his most important successor, Roberto Longhi. I also owe a debt of personal gratitude to Bernard Berenson, Florence; Cesare Gnudi, Bologna; Ludwig Goldscheider, London; Michel Laclotte, Paris; Ulrich Middeldorf, Roberto Salvini, Marchese Uberto Strozzi and Evelyn Vavalà Sandberg, all of Florence, who in various ways have helped me in my work and made it possible. I am grateful to R. H. Boothroyd, Verona, who translated this book from the German into English; and I would also like to thank the directors of the Emilian libraries and archives, the heads of museums in Europe and America and the owners of private collections, who were always willing to place at my disposal their material relating to paintings or sources.

Florence, June 1956   E.R.

CONTENTS

INTRODUCTION

COSIMO TURA, known also as Cosmè (1430–95),[1] enjoyed a high reputation during his lifetime, both as a man and as an artist, among the princes, courtiers, artists, poets and scholars of his native city of Ferrara. Laudatory descriptions such as 'praestantissimus vir Cosimus omnium nostri temporis pictor praestantissimus', 'nobile et eccellente homo M.° Cosimus del Tura, pictore famosissimo' or 'ingeniosus' are obviously something more than the customary courtly formulae and denote a deliberate and well-founded admiration for an outstanding fellow-citizen and contemporary. His works are praised with epithets such as 'diligenter et diligentissime factus' or 'elegantissime confectus'.

In his treatise on architecture (1460–4) Antonio Filarete mentions the then still young 'Gusme da Ferrara' side by side with some of the greatest and most celebrated men of the period: Fra Filippo Lippi, Piero della Francesca, Andrea Mantegna and Vincenzo Foppa. Raphael's father, Giovanni Santi, in his somewhat later 'rhymed chronicle' ranks Tura among such artists as Antonello da Messina, the Bellini brothers, Ercole Roberti and Melozzo da Forlì; he considers Cosimo Tura and Gentile Bellini as painters of equal merit.[2]

In recognition of his work Tura received from his chief patron, Duke Borso d'Este, a regular salary from 1452 on and many costly presents, while in 1457 he was given rooms in the ducal residence and in 1462 a house.[3] Ecclesiastics and prominent private citizens also gave him numerous commissions and for these Tura was in a position to demand high prices. The busy artist was thus able to accumulate considerable wealth and often lent large sums of money to others. In 1464 he bought with his own money a two-storied house with courtyard and loggia between the Via Centoversuri and the Via Boccacanale near Santo Stefano. On 14 January 1471, during a severe illness—before he had finished his most lucrative works, the painting of the great hall in Palazzo Schifanoia and of the chapel in the castle of Belriguardo near Voghiera—he stated in his first will that he wished to erect and decorate at his own expense a church in honour of Saints Cosmas and Damian, and to be buried therein; in addition to which he left generous legacies to the poor of Venice and to those who were nearest to him.

Tura's fame endured for some time after the death of Duke Borso in 1471. As a result of the pietistic tendencies of the new ruler, Ercole I, religious art enjoyed a new vogue and Tura devoted himself more and more to the painting of religious subjects, until about 1480 the general crisis put a temporary stop to the development of Ferrarese art. After this, Tura—the sole survivor of a declining stylistic tendency—failed to regain his pre-eminent position and Ercole Roberti, whose masterpieces in Bologna had made him famous, soon replaced him. We hear, it is true, of several other houses purchased by him, but after 1486 he withdrew to a tower on the city walls near the Porta Cosmaria, where he shared a dwelling and a studio with a painter named Teofilo. In 1490, in a written protest to Duke Ercole, Tura describes himself as a poor, sick man, no longer able to work and at a loss how to support himself and his family—by his housekeeper Orsolina he had had a son named Damiano Cosmo Maria. In 1491 he made his third and last will, after which we hear nothing more of him for four years—he died in April 1495 and was buried in the church of San Lorenzo at Ferrara. The chronicler who later recorded the event gave the artist a brief but eulogistic obituary notice.[4]

A few decades after his death only a dim memory of the great artist survived. In a conversation concerning Tura's masterpieces in the castle of Mirandola, people had difficulty in remembering the name of their creator. Tura's compatriot, the humanist Gregorio Giraldi (1479–1550), recalls vaguely having heard mention of a 'Cosman quendam', 'qui patrum nostrorum memoria nonnulla eius artis opera praeclara reliquit'.[5] In the first edition of his *Lives* (1550) Giorgio Vasari makes only a brief mention of Tura in connection with the painter Galasso, whose work we are no longer in a position to judge; Vasari mentions only two works by Tura and says that he presumably did not paint very many and was more important as a draughtsman than as a painter. In the 1568 edition the mention of Tura forms an appendix to the life of the sculptor Nicolò di Piero Lamberti, and Vasari describes him as a pupil of the painter Galasso and speaks of 'many works' which were better than those of his teacher.[6]

The name of Tura is rarely mentioned in the local chronicles and descriptions of monuments of the Baroque period, that same period which did not hesitate to destroy the master's works more recklessly than any earlier time. It is true that in 1702 Girolamo Baruffaldi wrote the first Tura monograph, of the greatest importance for scholars, but his manuscripts were read only by a few specialists and were not printed until 1836 and 1844. Baruffaldi considers our painter as one of the founders and the greatest representative of the old Ferrarese school, and posterity has confirmed his opinion, based on local patriotism, that the artistic significance of Tura's work extends far beyond the frontiers of Ferrarese art.[7]

Towards the end of the eighteenth century this esteem for Tura begins to gain ground. Vasari's opinion, often discussed by later writers, that Tura was merely a good draughtsman, is given a positive value in 1770 by C. Barotti, who considers Tura with his sure sense of style a forerunner of Albrecht Dürer. 'Ebbe egli (Tura) una maniera di disegnare assai anatomizzata, e con molta diligenza e finezza eseguì per fino l'ultime cose. Al suo piegare assimigliò molto Alberto Durero.' There is some truth in this statement, for Dürer copied numerous Ferrarese engravings, or else made free use of them.[8] Twelve years later Cesare Cittadella asserted that Heinrich Aldegrever, the manneristic Westphalian engraver, also followed Tura's style.[9]

In the first half of the nineteenth century the fame of the leading Ferrarese master became definitely established. The starting-point for a more or less thorough study of his works was provided by his share in the frescoes in the Palazzo Schifanoia at Ferrara; after having been long concealed by whitewash which gradually peeled off, they were completely freed in 1840 and were recognized as the work of Tura, thus confirming Baruffaldi's attribution. By the end of the century, L.N.Cittadella, Crowe and Cavalcaselle, Campori, Venturi and Gruyer, by their thorough investigation, study of the sources and stylistic criticism, had created an idea of Cosimo Tura which in its essential features has remained. The eccentric 'mannerist' became, for an age which no longer accepted the artistic and aesthetic ideals of classicism, one of the greatest artists of the Renaissance—one of the greatest because he was one of the most individual and spiritual.

II

The second half of the fifteenth century, to which Cosimo Tura's artistic activity belongs, can be considered, despite numerous crises, as a period of repose and enjoyment, and also—an inevitable consequence—of a certain decadence. The small Italian states of that time, among them those which had given the greatest encouragement to the arts, were in the hands of the intellectual and somewhat weary sons and heirs of energetic fathers. In defiance of the dangers threatening them, they held fast to the illusion of established legitimate authority and played the role of humane and highly cultured patrons, with a characteristic mixture of vanity and genuine thirst for culture, of passion and resignation. Skilful, or sometimes unsuccessful, diplomats rather than heroes, very subjective in their ideas, decisions and deeds, sensitive, melancholic and unstable, they transformed the grim castles of their ancestors into abodes of the Muses, or else, tired of the world and a life of action, withdrew to the peaceful solitude of their 'studios', which became their real throne-rooms.

The court of the Estes in Ferrara had an atmosphere and a way of life of its own, characterized by the cult of the unusual and of highly developed originality both in thought and in behaviour, which lent an unmistakable colour to the over-refinement of the prevalent courtly etiquette. On the one hand there was a liking for ironical, even frivolous and lascivious witticisms, on the other hand a desire for a type of 'scholarship' which tended towards the complicated and the obscure. Individuality and sentiment were held in reserve, as court etiquette demanded. The personal human element found satisfaction in a highly developed and sentimental appreciation of Nature. Sentimental release was sought in the gardens and parks of the palace on the outskirts of the city or in country villas; hunting and tournaments —an obvious echo of the 'romantic'—were popular. In the reign of Borso it was usual for people to dabble in all kinds of occult arts; bigotry and religious fanaticism gained the upper hand towards the end of the reign of Ercole I. A peculiar secretiveness was mingled with both these trends, and in many members of the Este family, and also in many leading courtiers of the time, we find traits which could be described as demonic.

It was in this atmosphere that the art of Cosimo Tura developed, an art which is a complete and characteristic expression of the atmosphere, in the middle of which stood the man Tura, who adapted himself to it. He possessed a solid middle-class authoritativeness, he was painfully exact in legal and financial matters, and strove in his bourgeois existence to achieve order, conciseness and reliability. If we examine carefully his unusually varied achievements, we obtain a picture of a careful, thorough and constantly diligent worker. Everything came easy to him and he worked very quickly. For the sculptural and pictorial decoration of the chapel in the castle at Belriguardo he was allowed five years, but he completed the work in two and a half, despite the fact that at the same time he worked in Ferrara, undertook several journeys and had one severe illness. Success and the demand for his services had as a consequence that he frequently accepted several heavy jobs at the same time, for example in 1469–71, when he had scarcely finished the painting of the organ door in Ferrara cathedral before he had begun work on the decoration of the large rooms at Belriguardo and in Palazzo Schifanoia, which he probably completed in the course of the same year 1471.[10]

It happened occasionally that Tura's works in their first form did not satisfy his patrons and had to be altered,[11] but this was never on account of faulty execution, which is never found in Tura's work. On the contrary, his unfailing carefulness was praised by his contemporaries and by all later writers and is confirmed by every work of his that has been preserved.

Designs for various crafts, allegories, religious pictures—these were the three chief branches of his activity. The first was probably the most important, though it is difficult to form an idea of what Tura achieved in this field owing to the lack of extant works. He was obviously a brilliant extemporizer, ready to employ his skill on such festive occasions as receptions, tournaments or solemn ceremonies. In such cases he painted flags and banners, arms and horse-trappings of wool or leather, as well as the costumes of the knights; he painted furniture and made designs for woven or embroidered fabrics, which were then executed by craftsmen. His designs for textiles—curtains, blankets, coverings for furniture, tapestries— were made during every period of his career and must have been one of his chief occupations. In addition he made models for goldsmiths and, at Belriguardo, worked as a decorative sculptor.[12]

The decorative element constitutes the great framework surrounding Tura's activity as a figure-painter, almost the only field of which we possess examples. This must be borne in mind if we are to avoid forming a one-sided idea of his art. The decorative intention must be recognized in Tura's painting, otherwise much would remain incomprehensible.

Nowhere, perhaps, during the Quattrocento was allegory treated more seriously or more individually than at the Estensian court. Poets, dramatists and artists showed equal zeal in devoting themselves to this genre, which found a natural place in the spiritual atmosphere of Ferrara. Allegory, invariably with a panegyric tendency and in most cases designed to form a eulogy of some ambitious ruler, gave its creator a welcome opportunity to display his wit and erudition, to be original and complicated and to set his listeners or spectators riddles which they would have difficulty in solving. Evidently they enjoyed these allegorical riddles and sharpened their wits on them. Obscure meanings and references kept their eager minds busy.

Cosimo Tura seems to have been a born painter of allegories, who possessed all the necessary qualifications. He was a cultured artist and proud of his culture. The highly disciplined, humanistic court milieu of the university city of Ferrara, in which this gifted son of a craftsman lived and rose to fame, awakened and encouraged all his faculties. Significant is Tura's predilection for little-known Latin quotations or for strange, mysterious ciphers, sometimes invented by himself, which are often found in his pictures. The scheme of his allegories was highly erudite and complicated; whether he evolved it himself or took it from some poet, he had to understand it and make it comprehensible with the means at his disposal. In 1465–7, when he decorated the library in the castle of Mirandola, he had to display an immense amount of erudition. In the Palazzo Schifanoia series (1469–71), his task defies definition, for here he tried to combine into one conception mythology, astrology, history and the events of his own time, philosophy and ethics, and to give of each twelve renderings—corresponding with the twelve months—and then to transform the whole into a hymn of praise for the ruling prince. The intellectual demands on him were overwhelming, but Tura was able to cope with them. He added other motives and these were what gave colour to the whole; he filled the work with his brilliant temperament, his wit, his irony and even frivolity, he gave it a demonic quality which his public understood and loved.

With his daring representations, which are not based on childishly innocent directness, Tura satirized one aspect of the spiritual life of his contemporaries, and he devoted himself to the task with all the assurance of a man of the world. The 'experienced hand' of the painter in administering light-hearted rebukes even won the praise of a poet, in the Latin elegy dedicated to Tura by the court poet Tito Strozzi: when it was a question of painting a 'Laïs', the poet thought at once of Cosimo Tura, and of him alone.[13]

Tura's religious art is equally unusual. In it we encounter traits which are difficult to explain and hardly ever to be found elsewhere. The artist deprives his Madonnas of the touching, intimate element found in the naively confidential Virgins painted during the Early Renaissance. They are idols, too pure and lacking in warmth; the Child Christs have nothing childish about them, but are ready to begin the work of salvation. These Madonnas are not intended for candid souls sure of their faith, but for anxious human beings. Tura's frequent renderings of the Mother with the Sleeping Child are by no means pious idylls. In his fervent inscriptions he tells us how he wants us to interpret them: 'Awake, Boy, that my soul may at last find beatitude!'[14]

Tura's saints are the complete expressions of inner problems, of an almost pietistic fervour and esotericism. They are monks full of a superhuman humility, ascetics and fanatics, with hectically reddened, sunken cheeks, feverish eyes and trembling hands. Here too, in these morbid psychopathic phenomena, there is a 'demonic' element.

The traditional symbols and attributes are given a curiously heightened meaning in Tura's pictures. The monkey in the tree in the Venice *Pietà* is an exhortation to the Imitatio Christi, but in this place and in this particular form, the symbol acquires an ironical, almost repulsive significance. And this is certainly not only a question of our own personal impressions; it was the pious-frivolous tone adopted in Tura's workshop when speaking of the highest things!

The extraordinary mind of Cosimo Tura had its roots in tradition, but he avoided being conventional and availed himself of every hitherto unused means of giving new life and significance to the traditional interpretations of his milieu. He remained an ordinary craftsman and felt himself to be an artist in the service of others, but he displayed all the freedom of genius. Restraint and independence, intellect and fantasy, piety and demonism combined to form a human figure, of which perhaps only we of today are able to judge the psychological importance.

There are two probable self-portraits of Cosimo Tura. In the lower field of the

September fresco, executed by Tura's own hand, in Palazzo Schifanoia, immediately to the right and behind the ambassador standing before Duke Borso, the head of a beardless man looks straight at the spectator. Position, attitude and the direction of the glance point to its being a self-portrait. Though this portion of the painting has been badly preserved, the essential features can still be discerned: a strikingly thin face with a low forehead, a very long chin, and ironical mouth and eyes. At that time Tura was about forty years old. The same head, but grown uglier and looking more sickly, is found again in the tapestries woven after Tura's designs in Cologne and Cleveland, which must date from the early 1470's. We see IIc, IIIc the same thin face with the over-emphasized, in this case curiously deformed, chin; the impertinent irony has been transformed into a tragical sourness, but the fundamental traits of the physiognomy are the same. That this was the appearance of the man whose nature we have tried to delineate, seems not improbable.

III

The development of Cosimo Tura's style was determined not only by his very pronounced individuality, but also by three other elements: the survival of mediaeval elements in Italian art during the first half of the Quattrocento, fructified by the steady influx of artists from the North and East, the courtly elegance of Pisanello's naturalism, and the 'mannerism' of one of the leading groups of artists during the first years of the Renaissance, a group which had one of its chief centres in the workshop of Francesco Squarcione at Padua. It is difficult to form a reliable idea of the individuality, quality and extent of the Late Gothic style in Ferrarese art. Students of the period are still to some extent groping in the dark as regards this point. We know the names of numerous artists who were active in Ferrara during the first half of the century and can deduce from the sources the names of those who were the most successful; but rarely can we establish a precise connection between the names and the works that have been preserved (before 1450 these show hardly any Renaissance elements).[15] The most important Ferrarese painter at this time seems to have been Antonio Alberti.[16] He was born in Ferrara but was active chiefly in Urbino and Perugia. In Urbino there is an important work by him, signed and dated 1439—the large polyptych from San Bernardino dei Padri Zoccolanti. This reveals to us an ingenious and powerful master of form, whose figures, energetically modelled, move freely and are full of expression. In Ferrara a fresco from a chapel in San Domenico, depicting the story of St. John the Evangelist, is attributed to Alberti.[17] These vivacious scenes, genre-like in their conception, have a fundamental tone of courtly elegance and produce a definitely Ferrarese impression.

Whether Tura was in close contact with Alberti is unknown—the latter died not later than 1449. But he was in close touch with another painter of Late or Post-Gothic stylistic tendency, one of those who bore the name of Antonio Orsini, known to have been active in Ferrara between 1432 and 1481. A conventionally gothicizing *Madonna*, signed by Antonio Orsini, is in a private collection in Venice. If we bear in mind that the painter of such antiquated religious pictures might be the same man who in 1472, together with the realistic portrait-painter Baldassare d'Este, valued Cosimo Tura's decorations in the chapel of the castle at Belriguardo, we can form an idea of the extent of the survival of late mediaeval tendencies in Cosimo's immediate artistic milieu.[18] Another laggard who remained firmly attached to the Gothic style was Francesco Pelosio, also a member of Cosimo's circle, by whom there exists in the Pinacoteca of Bologna a triptych revealing echoes almost of the Trecento, which bears the surprisingly late date of 1476. A curious mixture of mediaeval and Early Renaissance elements is found in another *Madonna,* which can also be attributed to Pelosio and was often copied; the Madonna's smile, almost a grimace, reminds us in part of the Trecento and partly of the courtly Tura. In Pelosio's large *Lamentation* from the convent of Corpus Domini, now in the Pinacoteca at Ferrara, reminiscences of Piero della Francesca are transferred back to Late Gothic.[19]

Other possible contacts are Nicolò Panizzato and Jacopo Sagramoro—both of whom, like Pisanello and Galasso, were predecessors of Cosimo Tura in the castle of Belriguardo.[20] Between 1428 and 1438 Nicolò and Jacopo, together with a painter named Domenico, with Benincasa, Simone d'Argentina and Andrea Costa da Vicenza, worked in the Casa Pendaglia at Ferrara,[21] from which building two frescoes were later removed to the Pinacoteca in Ferrara. One of these, a *Madonna with Saints Sebastian, James and Anthony,* reveals a certain free majesty of atmosphere and an amplitude in the composition and draughtsmanship which bring it into close relationship with the monumental cycle of *Sibyls,* unfortunately almost completely ruined, in a room of the Casa Romei in Ferrara. The latter wall-painting, with the proud and noble sovereignty of its style, is certainly the most important testimony to Ferrarese painting in the first half of the Quattrocento that has come down to us. In these aristocratic female figures we seem to see elder sisters of Tura's coolly sublime Madonnas.[22]

The account-books of the Ferrarese court contain a large number of names of foreign artists—Netherlanders, Frenchmen, Germans and Slavs. Foremost among them is Rogier van der Weyden, who was in Ferrara in 1449, enjoyed the favour of both the Marchese Leonello and of Duke Borso and executed a number of paintings for the court. According to Ciriaco d'Ancona, Ferrarese artists like

Angelo Maccagnino seem to have studied under Rogier, supposedly the art of painting in oil, but more probably that of a more objective and subtle rendering of nature.[23] Cosimo Tura also studied the works of Netherlandish painters, his early *Madonna* in the Accademia at Venice being a clear proof of this. The masters 8 who executed Tura's designs for woven fabrics and embroideries were for the most part Netherlanders or Frenchmen, for example Liévin de Bruges (Levino di Francia), Giovanni Mille di Francia, Rubinetto di Francia and Rinaldo Boteram de Bruxelles.[24] Among the Ferrarese miniaturists who followed Tura's style were some who were certainly of Flemish or German origin. In 1452 Tura worked in collaboration with one of the most important among them, Giorgio d'Allemagna, as he did with the creator of small sculptural works, Charles de Mauléon, known as Carlo delle Bombarde.

The continuing penetration of northern elements into the artistic circles in which Cosimo Tura worked, brought him time and again into contact with this school of art, and this explains the northern element in his style, which is undeniable and, as we have already seen, was emphasized by the earlier writers. Before Tura began working at Belriguardo, he had been to Brescia, to study a chapel painted by Gentile da Fabriano, and this at the express request of Duke Borso.[25] Jacopo Bellini[26] and Pisanello were also held in great consideration at the Ferrarese court.[27] Between 1432 and 1448 Pisanello visited Ferrara repeatedly, painting portraits and making likenesses for medals in addition to his religious paintings, among them, in 1445, an altar-piece for the castle at Belriguardo. The fidelity to nature and the elegant conception to be seen in his portraits of members of the Este family in Bergamo and Paris, were so completely in harmony with the prevailing 'tone', that Pisanello became the indispensable model for those painters who aspired to find favour at the Ferrarese court. Probably it was his nearness to Pisanello as a portrait-painter that first gained for Tura the esteem of the Estes; from Pisanello's portrait of the Marchese Leonello in Bergamo we can trace a direct link—through Giovanni da Oriolo's Leonello in London[28]—with Tura's first known work, the wonderfully elegant portrait of a youthful Estensian prince, now in New York. 1 Tura made Pisanello's precision of gesture his own and for a long time he filled his pictures with a careful choice of those realistic still-life details which are a characteristic of Pisanello's work: birds, squirrels, branches of fruit-trees and grapes, such as we see in the early *Madonna* in the Accademia at Venice and in the panels of the 8; *Annunciation* on the organ door painted in 1468–9.   19, 20, 24

The most important factor in the formation of Tura's style was, however, that early 'mannerism' which was a favourite tendency almost everywhere in Italy from about the middle until just before the end of the century. This 'mannerism' was directly derived from Late Gothic and it is easy to follow its progress until it culminated in the 'mannerism' of the High Renaissance.

For Tura the decisive model was probably the Paduan artist Francesco Squarcione. He and his earliest Northern Italian colleagues were born in the last years of the Trecento[29] and must have begun as Late Gothic artists. Squarcione's Lazzara altar-piece in the Museum at Padua—especially in the painting of the four side-panels—is in complete harmony with the flamboyant Gothic style of the carved frame which surrounds it. But in individual details the work already contains elements that remind us of Marco Zoppo (1433–78) and Cosimo Tura—the restless, decorative attitudes, the affected gestures, the sentimentally exaggerated, rather theatrical mimicry and also the individual nature of the draughtsmanship. The latter is characterized by a markedly elegant and sweeping ductus, a somewhat bombastic calligraphy, and a tendency to turn component details, especially the folds of the draperies, into geometrical, ornamental figures. In this picture Squarcione ventures to show a St. Anthony seen from behind; from the point of view of purport, this is senseless; the significance of the figure turning away from the spectator is probably purely formal, a device to give the figure a 'function', that of creating space. In Squarcione's pupils and followers, the craze for ornamentation goes so far that we find in the ever more abstract sweep of the folds the 'ear-shell' motive of sixteenth-century manneristic decoration, especially in one of 75 Cosimo Tura's late pictures, the *St. James* at Caen.

There were early followers of this manneristic tendency in Ferrara as well. Nicolò d'Allemagna, active in Ferrara from 1446, and Titolivio da Padova belong to the school of Squarcione. Pisanello's pupil, Bono da Ferrara, who was working in Siena in 1442 and therefore also belongs to the generation before Tura, painted in 1450 and probably in 1452 at Belfiore, and between these two dates he may have executed his signed fresco in the Ovetari chapel in Padua, which shows that he was a follower of the Squarcione school.[30] Even older than the above artists, and probably a contemporary of Squarcione, was the Hungarian Michele Pannonio, XVI born about 1395, who painted his *Ceres,* allegedly destined for Belfiore and now in Budapest, towards the end of the 1450's. It is a strange picture of almost demonic individuality in form and atmosphere, completely manneristic in the sense that Squarcione was manneristic, but at the same time executed in the most subtle manner, with a bold refinement in the choice of colours and unusual quality of draughtsmanship. A little later—during the first half of the 1460's—Tura added to 14 the allegorical cycle of which the *Ceres* forms part his *Venus,* now in London, and with this painting his art fuses completely with Michele's 'Squarcionesque' stylistic tendency and conception, towards which it had consistently tended from the beginning.[31] Another member of the 'Master of Belfiore's' circle was the Sienese Angelo Maccagnino, highly esteemed by both Leonello and Borso d'Este; known as Parrasio, he is first mentioned in 1439 and between 1447 and 1456 he began by painting two panels of a cycle of *Muses* for the studio at Belfiore, which are described by Ciriaco d'Ancona and which Tura, according to Lodovico Carbone, completed.[32] The Sienese background of painters like Bono da Ferrara and Angelo Maccagnino justifies the supposition that they were already well acquainted with the 'manneristic' style by the time they came to the part of Italy where Squarcione was working, and that they contributed on their own initiative to the diffusion of this style in Ferrara. Two masters of the generation born around 1400 were working in Siena at the time, the audacious Domenico di Bartolo and the bizarre Giovanni di Paolo, each of whom, in accordance with his own individuality and the artistic atmosphere of his native city, strove to achieve aims which were very close to those of Squarcione. Although no works are now known which can be attributed with certainty to Maccagnino, we may safely assume that he was a 'mannerist' and that he influenced Cosimo Tura and encouraged him to continue in his study of the 'Squarcionesque' style.

About a certain Galasso, often mentioned and said to have been Tura's first teacher, we know no more than we do about Maccagnino; the same may be said of the other Galasso who in 1451, together with Tura, made a valuation of some paintings by Jacopo Turola.[33] Whoever Tura's real teacher may have been, the 'manneristic' tone overshadows from the beginning all other tendencies to such an extent that we are bound to assume that this teacher was a follower of the 'Squarcionesque' tendency or of some other closely akin to it.

Though the beginnings of Tura's artistic education are still rather obscure, there is plenty of evidence of its later phases. For the most part it took place in Padua, Squarcione's home town, and Venturi thinks that the years 1453–5, for which we have no documentary evidence, must have been spent there.[34] In Padua Tura made a close study of the frescoes in the Ovetari chapel in the church of the Eremitani, on which the Muranese painters, Antonio Vivarini and Giovanni d'Allemagna, and followers or pupils of Squarcione such as Niccolò Pizzolo (about 1410–53), Ansuino da Forlì (known to have been active between 1434 and 1453), Bono da Ferrara, Andrea Mantegna and Gerolamo di Giovanni da Camerino (active between 1450 and 1463)[35] had been, and in part were still, working.[36] Of these, the most important after Mantegna seems—as Vasari also states—to have been Pizzolo and the latter had more influence on Tura than Mantegna himself, the metallic rigidity of movement in the latter's pictures being at that time incomprehensible for Tura. Pizzolo was a skilful stylist and was fond of those curiously

formal, but nevertheless concealed, elements that Tura also tried to express in his
pictures. In the course of his work in the chapel his manner achieved an outstand-
XA ing elegance and fluidity and in the tondi of the *Fathers of the Church* he anticipates the mature Tura to such an extent that one of them was actually attributed
to Tura himself.[37]

His Paduan impressions, however, did not really bear fruit until the 1460's, in
9–12 the altar-piece from Santa Maria della Consolazione, in which an echo of Pizzolo
28–31 can be detected, and in the Maurelius altar-piece from San Giorgio fuori, the pre-
XV served portions of which remind us of Ansuino da Forlì's fresco of St. Christopher
preaching. As time went on, Tura drew nearer and nearer to the Ovetari masters,
and in particular to Mantegna, clear instances of this being the Roverella altar-
piece and the late polyptychs. There is considerable resemblance to the Ovetari
Xc tondi in a drawing of a *Doctor of the Church* at Bayonne, attributed sometimes to
Tura and sometimes to Giovanni Bellini.[38]

The generation of 1430 appropriated in the widest sense the conceptions of the
older 'mannerists' of about 1400; they enlarged, ennobled and spiritualized them,
raising them to the level of a period style, which by 1470 dominated the field of
Italian painting and also that of sculpture. We find 'mannerism' everywhere
among the artists of Tura's generation: in Tuscany in Andrea del Castagno,
Alessandro Baldovinetti, Antonio del Pollaiuolo and Francesco di Giorgio; in
Umbria in Benedetto Bonfigli and Niccolò Alunno; in the Marches in the Crivel-
lis. In its most concentrated form, however, we find it in Northern Italy: at Padua
in Giorgio Schiavone and Bernardo Parentino, at Bologna and Venice in Marco
Zoppo and Bartolomeo Vivarini, at Ferrara in Baldassare d'Este, Francesco del
Cossa and many others. In Northern Italian sculpture it was particularly favoured
by Antonio Rizzo,[39] who was born in Verona and followed almost the same paths
as Tura, and by his collaborators and pupils in Venice, Padua and Lombardy:
Giovanni Antonio Amadeo, the brothers Cristoforo and Antonio Mantegazza, the
younger Giovanni Minelli. In the unexplored field of Ferrarese sculpture in Tura's
time there was likewise no lack of definitely 'manneristic' tendencies. They are to
be found in the work of Domenico di Paris, who executed the stucco decorations
in the ante-room of the great hall in Palazzo Schifanoia, as well as in the work of
artists who decorated various churches and palaces in Ferrara, among whom we
can mention sculptors like Sperandio, Gabriele Frisoni and Antonio di Gregorio.[40]
In Bologna Nicolò dell'Arca executed an important work of early manneristic
sculpture—the eccentrically dramatic group of the *Lamentation* in the church of
Santa Maria della Vita.[41] It is possible that the real source of this style is to be
found in sculpture—namely in those works of Jacopo della Quercia and Donatello

which were executed in Northern Italy. Bartolommeo Bellano and painter-sculptors like Squarcione and Niccolò Pizzolo provided the necessary link in Padua.

On the whole the artists of Tura's generation followed the same aim as he did and they sometimes found solutions which are inexplicably akin to his, since we do not know whether those who were nearest to him in style, Marco Zoppo and Bartolomeo Vivarini, ever came into actual contact with him. The problems were those of the time and artists of the same tendency dealt with them each in his own way. Influence may well have been reciprocal, but what really binds these artists together is a common higher factor—the 'manneristic' idea. In accordance with his rank as an artist, Cosimo Tura is at the centre of this movement.[42]

At the end of the century the young Michelangelo beheld with admiration the frescoes of Francesco del Cossa and Ercole Roberti—the greatest masters of Tura's wider circle—in the Garganelli chapel in the Metropolitana at Bologna, the 'maniera magnifica' of which impressed him very deeply—'Questa cappella, che avete qua', he said to his companions, 'è una mezza Roma di bontà!'[43] And Michelangelo's style shows us that these words, often repeated with pride, were spoken in all earnestness. The Emilian Parmigianino, whose fastidious art has become the synonym of the idea of 'mannerism', was the legitimate successor to the artistic heritage of Cosimo Tura, and he carried the ideas of Tura's time to their logical conclusion within the framework of Renaissance conception of form in the sixteenth century.

IV

At the beginning of Cosimo Tura's œuvre we must place the portrait of a youthful prince of the house of Este, now in New York. That it is generally dated later, is 1 due to an obvious and characteristic assumption: that at the very beginning of his career Tura would appear as an accomplished artistic personality, faultless and without any directly perceptible traces of tentative struggles; subsequently he showed so little 'development' that it would be difficult to bring his works into chronological order.

But on closer examination, and especially after careful comparisons, it becomes clear that of all Tura's pictures this is the strictest and most awkward in its construction, richer in the details of its draughtsmanship than any other, the most circumspect in the manner in which it is painted and the most cautious in its modelling. Here too we must acknowledge the 'connection' of this, probably the earliest specimen of his art, with that series of portraits of Estensian princes painted by Pisanello, Jacopo Bellini, Rogier van der Weyden,[44] Giovanni da Oriolo and also by Mantegna.[45] All these portraits were executed between 1441 (Pisanello, Bellini) and 1447–51 (Giovanni da Oriolo, Mantegna, and probably also Rogier van der Weyden).

The year 1451, the earliest in which Tura is known to have been active at the Estensian court, must also be considered as a likely date for the New York portrait.[46] The relatively primitive plan which Tura follows in this portrait— bust-length in strict profile against a neutral background surface—is the last recourse of all mediocre portraitists of the period. The more ambitious strove to achieve more complicated and livelier versions. Pisanello, for example, places a hedge of blooming flowers behind his model, which, apart from the naturalistic details, produces the effect of an ornamented carpet. In his double portrait of the Duke and Duchess of Urbino, painted in 1465 (Florence, Uffizi), Piero della Francesca contrives to lift the human figures out of their environment painted and to transport them into a vague and fragrant atmosphere.

The youthful Cosimo Tura, on the other hand, fitted himself into the framework of the inconspicuous normal style—in order to destroy it!

Tura makes use of all the refinement of his masterly craftsmanship, his cultivated taste, his comprehensive knowledge of form, obviously acquired with ease, and his differentiated psychology. This profile of a blasé boy breathes the pride of noble birth; the glance, beneath the raised, too finely drawn eyebrows, is full of lofty condescension despite the sitter's youth, while the mouth expresses scornful derision: as a work of art, it is the achievement of a half devout, half ironical submission to the reality of the model and his essence, and to the laws of a pictorial form which the artist has already tried and mastered and which he desires to achieve again. It is precisely that slight admixture of 'irony' that gives the picture its superiority; the masterly way in which the painter exceeds the conventionally prescribed measure as regards realistic details and delicate craftsmanship raises this apparently conventional little work to a level above that of all similar pictures.

About the same time Tura is said to have painted works for secular use: standards and banners; and he also decorated ceremonial helmets and painted and gilded caskets for the ruler. From 1457 on he made drawings and full-size coloured models on canvas for the use of weavers and embroiderers. His imagination and his talent for inventing patterns evidently enabled him to achieve considerable success in the designing and shaping of heraldic figures and ornamental motives, of elegant and ingenious decorations. His style of decoration during the 1450's must have been simpler, more restricted and more severe than that found in his later works.

Of actual pictures we hear nothing more until 1458, when Tura painted for a

Detail from Plate 81

Detail from Plate 47

remote and inconspicuous corner of Ferrara Cathedral a *Nativity*, which according to those who saw it consisted of numerous small figures. In the following year we find him among the artists working in the 'Studio' at Belfiore. His reputation, already great, and the quality of his previous works earned for him the title and function of a leading *depintore del studio*, as well as an increase in the fixed monthly stipend which for some time he had been drawing as one of the many more or less famous *salariati* of the Court. A brief statement that he was supplied with colours 'per depincere certe chosse del studio' is the only justification for the assumption that at that time Tura not only decorated furniture, curtains and other household articles, but also painted pictures. An important contemporary, Lodovico Carbone, states definitely that Tura finished the cycle of nine *Muses* for Belfiore which had been begun by Angelo Maccagnino.[32] Of all these works nothing has been preserved, but there exists a painted Allegory by Tura which for stylistic reasons can be assigned to the period when the work at Belfiore was completed (1463); this is the *Venus* now in London, generally assumed to have 14 formed part of the Belfiore decorations. Between the New York portrait of an Estensian prince and the London *Venus,* however, a number of other works must be inserted, all of which lie 'along the way' to the London picture, but are so closely akin to it, that the most restrained and therefore probably the earliest among them cannot be dated much earlier than 1460.

One of these works is now in Philadelphia and consists of two twin panels with single figures of John the Baptist and St. Peter, in a somewhat crude, Late Gothic 3–4 carved framework, standing like statuettes in a niche curved like the keel of a ship. Their authenticity has been disputed, because the possibility of their having been executed so early was denied.[47] Nevertheless it is quite logical to place them at this point in Tura's development. By that time the artist had mastered the problems of the older Squarcionesque school, treating and realizing them in an almost academic manner. He appropriated the curving style of draperies of these early 'mannerists', but instead of achieving flowing movement as was certainly his intention, he achieves an almost petrified rigidity. The ridges, sharply heightened with white, of the folds form a series of closely connected lines producing an effect of constrained ornamentation. The bodies are everywhere roundly modelled, but instead of being lifelike they are hard, as if they had been shaped on a lathe. By this time Tura had already reached the point when he could extend the fluid continuity of the manneristic line, making it a spatial factor instead of mere surface and outline of form. The linear pattern of the drapery folds lays great stress on the curves, which seek to make the bodies look round and to emphasize the protuberances and cavities of the forms. The landscape is constructed with a didactic purposefulness: a road or stone causeway, rising like a ramp, winds from the foreground into the pictorial plane in a geometrical curve.

Nevertheless, despite all their severity these little pictures are not without a certain intimate atmosphere. At the time Tura had already accepted as part of his artistic programme that expressive play of light and shadow with which he was later to achieve such astounding results. The two Saints in the twilit landscape are bathed in a physically perceptible, vibrating atmosphere. The system of sharply applied glittering lights covers the whole picture evenly and blends the cool reds, blues and greens to a more harmonious whole than in the portrait of the Estensian prince, in which the same range of colours is found. In the drawing of the lights a new factor appears, fundamentally identical with the concept 'manner', the cultivation of which was of prime importance for every 'mannerist'—the calligraphic factor. In this case it is still a circumspect, rather stiff and pedantic calligraphy, as impersonal as embroidery. But the artist has become conscious of the potential effectiveness of 'handwriting' and lays marked stress upon it. Tura never abandoned this method, but his 'writing' became ever freer, more assured and more expressive.

On the same stylistic level as these pictures of Saints is the half-length *Madonna*, tiny as a miniature, in front of a brownish mandorla bearing the signs of the zodiac, which is now in a private collection in Rome. It must have formed part of a larger complex and is perhaps connected with the Philadelphia *Saints*. With them it has in common a marked tendency to roundness in the delineation of the bodies, a similar style and certain motives in the carefully executed play of the folds and in the background landscape. Very close to these pictures is the *St. George on horseback* in the Asquith collection, which at the same time foreshadows Tura's horseman on the organ door in Ferrara cathedral.

Lastly there are two drawings from this period, to one of which—a *Christ*, a *Saint* or a *Marsyas*—Roberto Longhi was the first to draw attention.[48] The other is the sketch of a *Mercury* in Bayonne, hitherto attributed to Ercole Roberti.[49] However different the plan and atmosphere, the fact remains that formal conception and manner are identical. The *Mercury* confirms the correctness of Longhi's attribution, surprising though this at first may seem: here is a genuine Tura figure, such as we shall soon find again in a painting—in the little St. George of the Consolazione altar-piece. The previous dating of these two drawings, however, is far too late and they must be back-dated to the early 1460's; a later date would make it difficult to fit them into the scheme of Tura's development, but here, especially if we compare them with the two Philadelphia *Saints,* they form a harmonious whole.

What we have just said about 'calligraphy', becomes clearly visible in these drawings. Every detail reveals the artist's love of beautiful lines. Neither the *Mercury* nor the '*Christ at the Column*' is a nature study showing an earnest attempt 7, 5 to reproduce reality as objectively as possible both in the whole and in details. The mastery of reality has become as much a matter of course for the artist as the ability to achieve stylization of the form in the Squarcionesque sense, which no longer needs to be pedantically forced, as was previously the case. Tura is now able to 'juggle' with form. A connoisseur who looks at these drawings seems to be asked to admire and enjoy the sureness and elegance of the hand, the talent for intelligent implication. The control of manner has gone so far that, without losing any of its formal individual charm, it can express, in addition to beauty and elegance, also the casual and particular, and even the downright ugly. This nude bound to a 5 column or a tree, with the flabby breast of an old man and the almost hidden face of a satyr looking out from under the wildly falling hair, marks the whole breadth of a manner which is becoming more and more assured. The cloths enveloping the bodies of both figures like the spirals of a manneristic ornament flutter gracefully in the wind, the style of the drapery folds is freer than in the paintings; the direct medium of the drawing anticipates solutions which Tura the painter was able to achieve only later.

According to Beenken,[50] it was not until 1460 that the portrait of an Estensian prince (now in New York) left Rogier van der Weyden's workshop, and in fact it was just about this time that traces of Netherlandish influence began to appear in Cosimo Tura's works. The finest fruit of this influence was the little altar-piece of the Madonna in the Accademia at Venice, the panels of which are embedded in an architectural framework showing a supreme beauty of proportions, with noble I Early Renaissance ornamentation.[51] The whole is crowned by a somewhat carelessly carved lunette, with traces of Gothic in its decoration. The chief panel shows IIA a half-length Madonna with the sleeping Child, sitting behind a breastwork of 8 masonry. Grapes glowing with violet hang down from above, with gaily coloured birds perched among them. The greyish-blue twilight sky is covered by the fine gold lines of three figures of the zodiac: Virgo, Sagittarius and Pisces. Tura liked to scatter these astrological symbols about the backgrounds of his religious pictures, and they were not lacking in the little *Madonna* in Rome. In the *Annunciation* on the 2 organ door in Ferrara Cathedral planetary divinities, in the form of simulated 25–27 reliefs, adorn the walls of the Renaissance hall. The spirit of the Ferrarese Court becomes more and more evident.

In the main, however, Tura was thinking of Rogier van der Weyden when he painted the Venetian *Madonna*. The female type, with lofty white forehead and curved nose, the fragile, decorative hands reproduced down to the last detail, and in particular the white headdress with the hard, thin lines of its folds, all point to this. The colour scheme is cool, the flesh somewhat chalky. But the effect is more elastic, more playful and more calligraphic than in the works of the Netherlandish painter; it is more refined and more deliberate. Tura was too much of a mannerist to be able to become a primitive like Rogier; he rises to Rogier's level in order to surpass him. The intimacy of his conception of the Child contrasts with the unapproachable aloofness and fundamentally 'formal' appearance of the Mother. Rogier's candid accuracy and smooth execution is replaced by a delicate, but clearly discernible, 'handwriting' which plays a decisive part, a calligraphy which the Ferrarese artist intended us to enjoy, the charming little irregularities expressing something individual and discreetly personal—the expression of the temperament, the mood of the painter, of his own particular attitude towards the traditional subject as he interpreted it. And we can see how much the subject and its effect owe to calligraphy! In the somewhat stippled execution of the two angels in the lunette, in which we find once more the thin curling folds of the two drawings from the nude, there is a trace of improvisation and sketchiness which produces a remarkably developed and 'baroque' effect. We find the same effect in all the briskly recorded accessories in Tura's pictures; in the groups of tiny human figures in his backgrounds, on predellas and pillars, and this makes the pictures all the more attractive and interesting.

A return to earlier solutions of problems, frequent repetitions of the same motives in the details, often after long intervals of time, are repeatedly found in Tura's works and are probably due to the fact that they were based on a copious store of drawings. Such similarities must not mislead us into dating from the same period pictures in which they occur. For example, the motive of the sleeping Child

50 recurs in the much later *Madonna* of the Roverella altar-piece, and the slight back-

2 ward tilt of the Child's head in the Rome *Madonna* is repeated in a hitherto un-recognized work of Tura's, which must obviously have been painted after the

V Venice *Madonna*. This is the *Allegory of Charity* in Milan, which, originally the work of another hand, was partially repainted by Tura.[52]

As regards the subject, a 'Virtue', this Allegory is akin to the two Ferrarese

XIIB *Allegories* in the Strozzi collection at Florence—a *Prudentia* and a *Spes* (?).[53] The same applies to the composition—seated female figures, seen slightly from below. Stylistically, however, each of the three differs from the others and they must have been begun by three separate artists. The *Charity* was already in existence, though perhaps under another designation, when Tura undertook to supervise the continuation of the cycle. The antiquated upper portion of the figure has

Netherlandish features and the woman's head reminds us again of Rogier's models, which a not very talented artist was here trying to imitate.

Tura took care to see that the old and new panels of the cycle were made to harmonize with one another. The *Charity* was given a similar throne and almost the same background landscape as the *Prudence* and the *Hope*; over the back of the throne of *Charity* Tura hung the same cloth which we find again in the *Madonna* 80 *with blessing Child* at Bergamo. The partial alteration of the upper portion of the woman's body gave rise to disturbing discrepancies and it now seems formless and badly drawn. The lower half of the picture, however, was completely recast by Tura, who transformed it into a magnificent piece of painting, which must be restored to his œuvre. The cloth on the knee of the *Spes* also seems to have been slightly retouched by Tura, whose more energetic plasticity distinguishes it clearly from the flatness of the other parts. The *Spes* was the work of one of Tura's assistants, whom we shall find on several other occasions in the role of an imitator. The *Prudence,* on the other hand, is evidently an early work by Francesco del Cossa,[54] who later worked in Palazzo Schifanoia as an assistant or collaborator of Tura's. That Tura on other occasions repainted pictures by other artists or his own older works is proved by the contract of 1477–81 for the painting of Ercole I's 'Studio', which stipulates that four existing panels were to be altered by him.[55]

The three *Virtues* are likewise generally assumed to have formed part of the series of Allegories in the 'Studio' at Belfiore, though there is certain evidence only as regards the lost cycle of Muses by Angelo Maccagnino and Tura. The fragmentary remains of series of Allegories that have been preserved were probably destined for other rooms, though we do not know which. The style of all three pictures points to the early 1460's. The incredible number of Estensian castles which were decorated at that time and throughout Borso's reign, and the unreliability of the information about them, make a more exact identification and localization of the cycle of Virtues impossible.

In contrast to his earlier pictures, the *Charity* repainted by Tura reveals an V advanced stage of stylistic development. The modelling is firmer and more powerful, and at the same time gentler and more spacious; the very manneristic draughtsmanship in the figures of the three dancing children has a certain bizarre element; the style of the folds in the blue mantle of the woman anticipates that angularity which may have been Netherlandish in its origin, but in the mature Tura assumes a completely individual character. The *Charity* stands midway between the Venice *Madonna* and the stylistically already very angular *Venus* in London. The 8, 14 link between the two last-named pictures is provided by another allegorical work,

which hitherto has been almost completely neglected and perhaps not yet cor-
rectly identified.

VIIA   This is the drawing of a standing female figure, probably Vesta, in the Albertina
in Vienna, which is there attributed to a Northern Italian engraver and dated about
1500.[56] It is more likely that it is a drawing made by Tura in the early 1460's,
revised to such an extent that it is now hardly recognizable. The conception of this
Sibylline figure has deliberate grandeur. The curiously spiral folds of certain por-
5, 7   tions of the draperies are familiar to us from Tura's two early drawings, and the
motive of the arm hanging down almost rigidly, with the hand outstretched, is
V   very nearly a repetition of that seen in the Milan *Charity*. In the style of the folds,
insofar as it is possible to form a reliable judgement, there are definite traces of that
14   angularity which completely dominates the London *Venus*. The profile, still
visible, of the left leg with the exaggerated outward curves of the thigh and shank
and the deep recess at the knee, to which the robe seems to be sticking, are found
83   in a more rigid and abstract form in Tura's late *St. Anthony* in Modena, painted
in 1484. That he was the author of this drawing—probably a preliminary sketch for
another series of Allegories in the early 1460's—can hardly be doubted. The
amateurish revision has robbed it of all its effectiveness.

The firm plasticity of the flesh in the repainted portion of the *Charity* and the
nervous restlessness of the hard style of the folds in the drawing of Vesta in Vienna
are combined in the chief picture of the *altar-piece of the Madonna* from the church
9–12   of Santa Maria della Consolazione in Ferrara. The date and reassembling here
proposed differ so greatly from those hitherto suggested, that they need further
12   explanation. The chief picture in Ajaccio is held to be Tura's latest work and Longhi
dates it about 1490.[57] It is considered to be an (unsuccessful) attempt of an ageing
master to adapt himself to the style of younger artists, in particular Ercole Roberti,
and as evidence of failing creative powers. Proofs of this are stated to be the peculiar deformations of the bodies, an alleged stiffness of expression and the one-time
monotony of the colour-scheme, though when the picture was partially cleaned in
1956, it was revealed that the colouring was remarkably bright. It is my opinion
that it is extremely close to the paintings and drawings we have just been discussing,
but a long way from Tura's 'petrified' abstract late style, a characteristic example
83   of which is the *St. Anthony* in Modena, painted in 1484. From the Ajaccio *Madonna*
12, 14 to the London *Venus* is but a short step. The *Venus* with its exaggeratedly large
head and hands is no less 'deformed', the mask-like expression of the face is just
as stiff and the colour-scheme likewise heavy and subdued.

To this painting of the Madonna must be added, as paintings originally on the
frame, three panels with single figures, a *Virgin of the Annunciation* in Rome, a

St. George in Venice and a *St. Maurelius* in Milan. All of these belong to the same 9–11
stylistic stage as the main picture, with which they also have in common the
architectural background motive of double pillars in various colours. They are so
clearly attuned to the *Madonna* that it is difficult to understand why this so obvious
connection has never been noticed. The little *St. Maurelius* in Milan is an example
of brisk, succulent improvisation, brilliant in its colouring. The *St. George* is considerably stiffer, but these are variations which it is possible to find juxtaposed in
the works of any painter.

With the Vesta drawing in Vienna and the Consolazione altar-piece Tura passes
from a careful firmness and tranquillity to almost violent movement; a kind of
'Storm and Stress' period ushers in his maturity. Taken as a whole the composition
of the chief picture is, it is true, perfectly symmetrical, almost Byzantine in its 12
regularity. Three figures, unrelated to one another, stand stiffly erect side by side;
the middle figure, the Madonna with the Child nibbling cherries, is one step higher
than the two Saints on either side, St. Jerome and St. Apollonia. Symmetry of this
kind, however, is not due to academic awkwardness, but to the deliberate intention of an artist sure of its effect; Tura is merely playing with the more antiquated
form of composition. The stiff attitudes are nothing but a careful rendering of
suppressed movement. One has the impression that the figures are swaying on their
feet, as if offering resistance to a strong wind, which is caught up by their flowing
robes, tugs at them and presses them against their limbs, the powerful plasticity of
the latter showing through the draperies. As the 'grace-notes' play about a simple
musical theme, so do the thin, crumpled folds enclose the solid basic forms in a
wild confusion of movement. The freedom of the early drawings is here trans-
planted into a painting.

This new tendency towards explosive movement is applied even to that most
tranquil of all themes, the portrait. The *Portrait of an unknown man* with Mephis- 16
tophelian features, often wrongly excluded from Tura's œuvre and attributed to
Marco Zoppo, now in Washington,[58] belongs to the same stylistic stage that Tura
achieved in the Consolazione altar-piece. The extent of the artist's development
during a full decade can be judged if we compare this portrait with the likeness,
apparently archaic in its tranquillity and stiffness, of the Estensian prince, dating
from the early 1450's. Even the outline of the face is in uneasy gliding movement,
only the surface retains the usual firmness and smoothness. The contrast, here
too, is a deliberately used means towards the achievement of effect; in Tura movement is not chaos, but energy. At this point in his development the London *Venus* 14
becomes a possibility and in fact it must have been painted during the first half of the
1460's.

Although the goddess sits on her grotesque throne of dolphins like a statue in its niche, the picture is remarkably agitated and alive. This niche with its almost monstrous decorations is the most impressive and the clearest evidence of Tura's decorative style at this time and in the years that followed; we have to return to it repeatedly, if we wish to form a concrete idea of Tura's subsequent work in the field of craftsmanship. The ornamental dolphins look as if they were made of metal, or of gold, their eyes are like fiery sparkling rubies; but on the other hand they seem to be alive and inspire fear. Their bodies bristle with spines and points, their mouths full of teeth sharp as razors are greedily open, their spiky fins and tails thrash about them dangerously.

Venus sits on her throne not as the goddess of love and beauty, but like a cold-blooded demon; one of her arms rests challengingly on her knee, the mask-like, smooth face with its staring doll's eyes is thrown back with a defiant gesture. The folds of the reddish mantle tumble down among the petrified bodies like a mountain torrent; on the ground they pile up in a mighty overflow, boiling up restlessly and bursting asunder, angular and pointed like glass. By means of deeply indented shadows and sudden lights the continuity of the surface is broken up; the picture is permeated by a wild, harshly accented rhythm of movement; the effect is not only optical, but one might almost say acoustic—we seem to hear it crackling and splintering.

The drawing of *Charity* in Berlin,[59] dating from the same period, must be compared with the two earliest drawings, if we wish to form an idea of the transformation of style. The elegant calligraphy has vanished; here nothing flows, everything is breaking. Curves are reduced to simple straight lines, bends to breaks or corners. Here Tura models the nude and the draperies, no longer with careful hatching adhering closely to the curves of the form, but with short, almost clumsy parallel strokes, which are kept as straight and perpendicular as possible and follow carefully the plastic proportions of the form. This Charity is an equally terrifying being, with stress laid on the ugly features, the sullen glance, the thin angular limbs and a ridiculous pair of wings. The child at her feet is grasping greedily at the symbolic flames, but this allegorical incarnation of human love is aloof and seems to be jealously holding back the charity she ought to dispense. Naturally, the allegory is not intended to have this absurd ironical significance, but it produces a very similar effect.

This drawing, too, probably had some connection with a cycle of pictures. As regards subject-matter, the half-naked woman could be fitted into the series of seven 'femine nude'—presumably the liberal arts, but with an artist like Tura they might well have been individual interpretations of the Cardinal Virtues—on which he worked between 1477 and 1481. By order of Duke Ercole, he had, for reasons we do not know, to alter four already existing panels, which may have been earlier works of his own. It is as easy to assume that the Berlin drawing was a study for one of these older *Allegories,* as it is to imagine what Ercole, about the year 1480, would have disliked in this coarse production.

V

At the time, however, such unusual experiments as these of Tura's were in accord with the taste of the 1460's and especially with that of the then reigning Duke Borso. The success they brought him is revealed by his steady adherence to the style and conception of the Berlin *Charity* and the London *Venus* until the end of 13, 14 Borso's reign in 1471. The period of veiled but perceptible seeking ends with the *Venus* and the first period of Cosimo Tura's maturity now begins.

Not as a proof of failure in his home city (as is generally assumed), but rather as an outstanding success elsewhere, must we consider the fact that Tura, after finishing a few commissions for household articles, left Ferrara in 1465 and went to the castle of Mirandola, where Count Francesco I Pico entrusted him with the considerable task of decorating the library. From a dialogue written by Lelio Gregorio Giraldi,[60] we can form an idea of the subjects and the arrangement of the paintings which were executed. There seem to have been twenty-four pictures, contained in six panels.[61] The arrangement was similar to that of the still existing series of the Months in Palazzo Schifanoia at Ferrara: three friezes one above the other, in this case rounded off at the top by a semicircular lunette. In the friezes Tura depicted all the most celebrated authors in every branch of literature, from the mythical beginnings down to the Middle Ages. Two fields were left free for pictures representing the literary life of the time. The compositions probably consisted of many-figure groups, shown 'in action' as they are in Raphael's *School of Athens.* The six lunettes contained mostly 'Trionfi', that is to say allegorical processions of personages of more general importance—great patrons and divine protectors or incarnations of the various branches of literature. Tura's manner of rendering such 'Trionfi' can be seen in the Schifanoia frescoes, where triumphal processions are also to be found in the upper compartments. The pictures were arranged in an order based on historical grounds (see the diagram, overleaf).

Of the Mirandola paintings, which covered three or four walls of the library and were enframed in a rich decorative ensemble—perhaps fresco or inlaid wainscoting—nothing has been preserved. They were doubtless one of Cosimo Tura's most important works.

I	II	III	IV	V	VI
PROFANE AND RELIGIOUS POETRY	GREEK HEROIC POETRY	ROMAN POETRY	ROMAN EMPERORS AND CHRISTIAN POETS	DRAMATIC POETRY	LYRIC AND EPIGRAMMATIC POETRY
Triumph of Poetry	The Seven Sages of Greece and Greek elegiac poets	Mythical Roman poetry	Roman Emperors	Triumph of Tragedy and Comedy	The oldest Greek lyric poetry
Old Testament Hebrew poets	The great Greek philosophers	The oldest Roman poets and authors of epics	Early Christian poetry	Older Greek dramatic poetry	Later Greek lyric poets and satirists
Mythical Greek poets	The seven great poets of Greece	Roman elegiac poets	*Left free for later representations of great contemporary writers*	Later Greek dramatic poetry	Roman lyric poets
The Sibyls	Love poetry of the Greeks	The Roman Satirists		Roman dramatic poetry	Epigrammatists

Library of the Castle of Mirandola: Scheme of Decoration; after Hermann in the Vienna Yearbook, 1898, XIX, p. 207f.

Another lost work is the decoration of the Sacrati family chapel in San Domenico, executed by Tura after his return to Ferrara at the end of 1467. According to those who saw them, the walls of the chapel were completely covered with many-figure frescoes, the subjects comprising 'the whole of the New Testament'. We may suppose that the walls were divided according to a given scheme into numerous compartments of equal dimensions, the uppermost being semicircular in shape or forming pointed arches. These compartments would certainly have contained many-figure compositions showing events from the Life of Christ; at the top there were probably single figures of the Evangelists. The chief item in the ornamentation of the chapel was an altar-piece, likewise painted by Tura, showing the Adoration of the Magi.

Serafino Serafini had executed paintings in San Domenico in 1373, as had Antonio Alberti about 1440.[62] Tura finished the Sacrati chapel in 1468, and in 1471–2 Baldassare d'Este decorated another chapel in the church in a similar way; this was the Ruffini chapel and a valuation of the work was made by Cosimo Tura.[63] Vasari, who mentions the Sacrati chapel as one of the few works by Tura he knew, also states that there were frescoes by Lorenzo Costa in the choir of San Domenico which already possessed magnificent Gothic stalls by Giovanni Baisio (1384). Lastly, according to Baruffaldi, the church also contained a number of statues of high quality, so that it must have been a veritable museum of all that was best in old Ferrarese art.[64] By 1621 Tura's frescoes had already been covered with whitewash and during the complete restoration of the church in 1717 they disappeared for good. Nor do we know the whereabouts of the altar-piece, which Baruffaldi says Tura merely repainted. The *St. Charles* by Scarsellino still in San Domenico shows nothing to justify the chronicler's statement that Tura's *Adoration of the Magi* might be beneath it.[65]

Another work by Tura, however, has been preserved, and that is the door of the organ in Ferrara Cathedral, with its monumental paintings executed in 1468–9. Here for the first time we see Tura as a monumental painter, and he shows himself to be just as capable of dealing with this very large format, as with the normal medium size or the small pictures he generally preferred. The grandeur of the subject-matter is in correspondence with the dimensions. 17–27

In the *St. George and the Dragon* on the outside of the door-wings the explosion of movement is tremendous and all-pervading. Here all trace of symmetry has vanished, the construction has no uniformity and the direction of movement in the composition is unilateral. Everything is in movement and in transition. In this picture space does not end on reaching the surface of the painting, in fact it seems to start from it, for the figures seem to be rushing out of the surface towards us; no limits are set and there is no neutralizing counter-movement. 17–18

This is not only a far more agitated, rapidly moving picture than all the previous works, it is also a 'louder' one, which we cannot help 'hearing'. We hear the sharp clash of the weapons, the rhythmical beat of the horse's hoofs, the terrified neighing of the charger, the hiss of the dragon; the silk robe of the fleeing princess, inflated by the wind, seems to crackle and rustle.

In this explosive picture the only co-ordinating factor is the rhythm, which transforms all the movement into a measured dance. Considered in the abstract it is a system of lines, which either correspond or produce an artistic contrast, intertwining and disentwining. This rhythmic dance measure is one of the most important elements in Tura's compositions.

In contrast, the *Annunciation* on the inside of the door-wings is—in accordance with the requirements of the subject—completely tranquil and harmonically even. Here again we have a deliberate contrast, for this *Annunciation* is one of Tura's 'quietest' pictures. The architecture of the hall in which the scene takes place is classical Early Renaissance. Here all movement is confined to the soul, but 19–20 nevertheless it makes itself felt. No artist, either before or after Tura, ever conceived a Madonna of the Annunciation like this, and he uses all his acute, penetrating psychology in order to achieve something different. Here there is no trace of the usual drastically expressed fear, of the childishly devout and silent humility: the saintly grief of Mary because she has been chosen and therefore excluded, is expressed in this unhealthily sensitive face with the lofty forehead, in the huge sunken eyes and in the pale transparent skin.

These pictures painted on canvas also have a somewhat monotonous colour-scheme. The general tone is cool and dark, the robes of the principal figures with their red, madder and blue shades blend with the whole; only a few bright reds stand out: the little slippers of the women, the bridle of the horse, the robes of a few figures in the background of the *St. George and the Dragon*. On the whole the painting is subdued chiaroscuro, sometimes glittering with cleverly applied tempera lights reminding us almost of Watteau. The calligraphy, astonishingly subtle despite the gigantic format, is one of straight lines and angles. The folds fall almost perpendicularly from the sleeve of the fleeing princess, and they lie almost horizontally over the supported thigh of the Angel of the Annunciation. Within these firm basic lines, however, there is a wealth of restless movement, a breaking and shattering which takes no account of what would be physically possible.

Even more peremptory is the angular style of the *St. Maurelius altar-piece,* which Tura painted for the chapel of the same name in the church of San Giorgio fuori le mura at Ferrara. The few portions of this altar-piece which have been preserved—two tondi representing the condemnation and the execution of the Saint, 28–31 now in the Pinacoteca at Ferrara—show clearly that it belongs to the same stage in Tura's development as the frescoes in Palazzo Schifanoia. The actual date of its execution was probably shortly before the painting of the organ doors.[66]

In contrast to most of the pictures so far discussed, the colour-scheme of these tondi is cheerful, one might almost say bright—unbroken local tones stand side by side. The compositions have a certain stiffness, and that of the execution scene looks as if it has been deliberately constructed. The same stiffness is found in the tranquil, erect attitudes and gestures of the thin, doll-like figures and in their jerky movements. A perfect example of the 'angular style' is the flag planted upright exactly in the middle of the execution scene, the harsh red making it look as if it were not made of cloth, but of crackling paper. The pattern of the folds of the knight's mantle in the execution scene is made up of wilful perpendicular, horizontal and diagonal lines.

Tura's calligraphy has become strangely lapidary; more and more it abandons the elastic Squarcionesque roundness and it becomes more and more like the style of a wood-engraving, though it is true that in doing so it achieves a rare decorative charm. This may have been the result of the many frescoes for the decoration of rooms that Tura painted about this time. Perhaps in the Sacrati chapel he found that this calligraphy, which he also used in the Schifanoia frescoes, provided the necessary decorative effect. To this period also belongs the *Madonna in the Garden* 32 in Washington, the extreme example, among Tura's panel-paintings, of the angular style. As a logical consequence of his previous development and a direct stylistic forerunner of the Schifanoia frescoes, the date of which is certain, this little picture must have been painted at the end of the 1460's and can certainly not have been his first work, dating from about 1450, as is generally assumed.[67] Against the latter dating we have the quite effortless, almost routine, matter-of-course way in which the straight folds, breaking into geometrical angles, are placed on the surface with rather broad strokes of the brush. The colouring is bright, but that is also true of the St. Maurelius tondi, the inventive faculty—especially as seen in the ornamental vegetation of the background or in the miniature-like, heraldic cloud behind the white head of the Madonna—is old-fashioned; but with Tura that does not signify much more than a caprice. Capricious, too, is the fanciful idea of the plastic application of that Gothic ornament in the shape of a T or an M which hovers lightly above the halo, making a caryatid of the Madonna and enframing, like a 33 kind of parenthesis, an Annunciation consisting of two tiny half-length figures.

The frescoes in Palazzo Schifanoia, begun in 1469, find their natural place at this point in the development of Tura's work.

About half of the paintings in the large hall on the upper floor of the palace have been preserved. On the west and south walls there remain only a few more or less obliterated traces, otherwise almost empty surfaces. Nine out of the total of nineteen main paintings must thus be considered as lost, but the general lines of these can be reconstructed on the basis of what is left.[68]

A stylistic examination of what remains shows that five artists must have taken part in the work.[69] The sources give us the names of two of these—Francesco del Cossa and Baldassare d'Este.[70] Cossa's share, however, is easy to define; according to his own statement it included the three pictures of months on the east wall—March, April and May. Only in the lower portion of the *May* can a decisive intervention on the part of another master be detected. On the north wall the style of a not very talented painter is predominant; the coarse mannerism which is his particular characteristic and his preference for squinting eyes in the human faces point clearly to Antonio Cicognara of Cremona.[71]

According to the sources, immediately after the completion of the frescoes Baldassare d'Este repainted a large number of heads and busts; to judge from the style of these repaintings, parts of which can still be recognized, the beautiful figure of a horseman beside the *June* must also be attributed to Baldassare.[72] The west wall, together with parts of the pictures on the south wall, seem, on the other hand, to have been the work of one and the same master, who decorated the so-called Sala del Pane in the castle of Bentivoglio (near San Giorgio di Piano) with paintings of secular subjects, obviously inspired by the Schifanoia frescoes.

34–42   Of the pictures of the months, *September* and the Cossa frescoes are the most important. The style of the *September* is found again at several scattered points: in the intermediary picture beside February, in the recumbent figure of the Zodiac
43 Virgo in the middle row of August and below on the right in the July. In other words, in a complete picture of a month, in an intermediary picture, in one of the figures on the middle row against a neutral background surface, and in one of the 'loggia scenes' of the bottom rows. All the other painters adhered strictly to the programme of a picture of the month, an intermediary picture and a 'loggia scene'. The head of the Virgo was almost literally repeated in that of the standing decan divinity next to it. The compartments executed by the painter of *September* were thus veritable models, specimens of all the projected types of pictures which the other painters had to follow. This fact, and the high quality of the September fresco, show that whoever painted it was the leading master when the hall was decorated between 1469 and 1471 (see diagram, pp. 30–31).

The leading master cannot have been any other than Cosimo Tura himself. This attribution is not new; on the contrary, it is the oldest known and was made about 1700 by Baruffaldi, who was expressing the certainty based on traditional evidence.[73] The nineteenth century took a narrower view of its authenticity than the Baroque period, claiming that, though Tura was the leading master, he painted only very little himself.[74] The September fresco was included among this, but unfortunately it was brought into relationship with the August picture, one of the weakest in the hall. In 1885 Venturi still maintained that Tura was the leading master and that in addition to the September (and August), the lower row of the July also revealed his influence more clearly than the other portions;[75] shortly afterwards, however, he asserted that for an external reason the idea of Tura's participation must be abandoned, the reason being that just at that time Tura was working at Belriguardo.[76] This is not a valid reason, for we have seen that Tura was a quick worker and often accepted several commissions concurrently; in fact, he completed the work at Belriguardo in half the stipulated time. Moreover, he had three assistants in Palazzo Schifanoia and two at Belriguardo. Nevertheless the rejection of Tura has been supported by subsequent writers; Longhi and Ortolani both describe the *September* as a youthful work of Ercole Roberti, despite the fact that in works which are known with certainty to be by Roberti, there are no stylistic parallels whatsoever which would justify this attribution.[77] Ortolani at least admits that in the Hall of the Months drawings and cartoons by Tura may have been used.

In reality, almost every portion of the September fresco reveals parallels with works known to be his. To cite a few examples: the noble, aristocratic profile of the horseman in the middle of the bottom row is almost identical with that of the youthful prince in New York, and this resemblance can be followed even in details of type, expression, conception of form and style. The triumphant divinity on the car drawn by apes at the top is, from an artistic point of view, akin to the drawing of *Charity* in Berlin, and the same applies to the wailing man in the right-hand compartment of the middle row, if we compare it with Tura's *St. Sebastian* in Berlin. The cyclops seen from behind in Vulcan's forge can be compared with the warrior turned away from the spectator in the tondo of the condemnation of St. Maurelius, the cyclops on the left with Tura's *Hercules* drawing in Rotterdam. The unusually feminine putti above the love scene remind us strikingly of the Child in the little *Madonna* in Rome. The quick dance-step of the movements, the affected gestures, the peeling rocks, the monotony of the colour-scheme, the chiaroscuro (even in a fresco!), the refined irregularity of the method of composition—parallels to all these things can be found in Tura's panel-paintings and drawings.

The spirit of the whole, in particular that of the *September*, is worthy of Tura and characteristic of him.

We have already mentioned the complicated nature of the Schifanoia scheme of decoration. The subject-matter comprises an interesting combination of all the imaginable and hitherto known ways of representing the months in the form of pictures. We find the twelve great gods of Olympus as patrons of the twelve months according to the system of Manilius, the twelve signs of the Zodiac, the thirty-six decan divinities and the traditional labours of the months (mostly agricultural).[78] But they are enriched with other and new ideas: to the normal labours of the months are added others of a 'lofty' nature, spiritual and artistic. The whole is raised from the level of an allegory of Time to that of an allegory of the Virtues and is transformed into a clever flattering panegyric of the ruler and patron Borso d'Este. Twelve main virtues are here glorified: Justitia, Majestas, Religio, Providentia, Fama, Caritas, etc. The Olympic and planetary gods who pass by in triumphal processions represent, encourage—and sometimes imperil—these virtues; they imperil them in order to show the ethical qualities and merits of the glorified ruler in a better light as their preservers. Not only the old gods, but also the astronomical divinities become Virtues in accordance with their particular significance, and to

EAST WALL

	May	April	March
	Cossa and Unknown	Cossa	Cossa
	Cossa	Cossa	Cossa
	Unknown	Cossa	Cossa
	Unknown		

NORTH WALL

September	August		July		June		
Cicognara	Tura	Cicognara		Cicognara	Cicognara	Cicognara	
Cicognara	Tura	Cicognara Tura	Cicognara	Cicognara	Cicognara	Cicognara	Baldassare
Cicognara	Tura	Cicognara		Cicognara	Tura		
Cicognara							

WEST WALL

	December	November	October
	Unknown	Unknown	Unknown
	Unknown	Unknown	Unknown
		Unknown	
	Unknown		

SOUTH WALL

	February		January		
Tura	Unknown	Unknown	Unknown		
Tura	Unknown	Unknown	Unknown	Unknown	
Tura	Unknown				
Unknown					

Palazzo Schifanoia, Hall of the Months
Diagram showing the division of the work among the various painters.

Palazzo Schifanoia, Hall of the Months: Subject-matter of the Frescoes

EAST WALL

	May	April	March
	Triumph of Apollo Liberal Arts	Triumph of Venus Pairs of Lovers	Triumph of Minerva Scholars—Weavers etc.
	7th, 8th, 9th Decan Gemini	4th, 5th, 6th Decan Taurus	1st, 2nd, 3rd Decan Aries
	Haymaking Hunting	Races Borso and Hunting Jester	Hunting Borso administering Justice

(Majestas?)   (Justitia)

NORTH WALL

		September	August		July	June	
Enemy Invasion		Triumph of Vulcan Smithy, Mars, Venus	Triumph of Ceres Ploughing, Harvesting	Court-yard of Castle	Triumph of Jupiter —Cybele Wedding— Heathen Priest	Triumph of Mercury Musicians— Merchants	Horse-men
		19th, 20th, 21st Decan Libra	16th, 17th, 18th Decan Virgo		13th, 14th, 15th Decan Leo	10th, 11th, 12th Decan Cancer	
		Borso and Hunters Ambassador	Hunters—Borso and Ambassador		Hunters—Borso and Peasant (Beggar?)	Borso and Hunting Steward Cortège	

(Providentia)   (Religio?)   (Plutus?)

WEST WALL

	December	November	October
	Triumph of Vesta	Triumph of Diana	Triumph of Mars or of Fame
	28th, 29th, 30th Decan Capricornus	25th, 26th, 27th Decan Sagittarius	22nd, 23rd, 24th Decan Scorpio
	Courtyard of Castle	Cortège of Hunters	Courtyard of Castle

(Caritas)   (Fama?)

SOUTH WALL

	February		January	
Horsemen	Triumph of Neptune	Tournament	Triumph of Juno or of Janus	Borso proclaimed Duke of Ferrara
	34th, 35th, 36th Decan Pisces		31st, 32nd, 33rd Decan Aquarius	
	Hunting Cortège Borso enthroned		Worshippers	

(Auctoritas?)

Palazzo Schifanoia, Hall of the Months: Subject-matter of the Frescoes.

characterize them the artist takes from the old lists only those qualities, attributes and tones which happen to coincide with those of the usual personifications of Virtues and Vices, omitting all the others. In the pictures in the lowest rows, reserved for actual contemporary events, the protagonist, Duke Borso, appears in person. We see him performing some act of government, giving practical effect to the Virtue forming the subject of the picture: such scenes are generally placed in or in front of a loggia, which enframes them and throws them into relief. In the intermediate pictures, which form a coherent 'sequence' running behind the pictures of the months and becoming visible only at irregular intervals, historical events are represented having a direct connection with the preceding or following 'Virtue', illustrating and confirming it.

Identical in every way was the system followed by Giorgio Vasari when, in his *Ragionamenti*, he explained his allegories of the months in the Palazzo Vecchio at Florence as a series of Virtues and the whole as the 'Ruler's Year'.[79]

In carrying out the project Tura used all his mind, his wits and his 'demonic' powers. Nowhere are these more clearly visible than in the painting he executed himself—the *September*—in which the divinities of Fire and War are shown amidst scenes of wantonness, debauch and violence—a martial panorama, the individual episodes of which are probably allusions to political and economic disputes between Ferrara and Venice.[80] This is the most melancholy and the least innocent picture in the whole cycle. The effect is due mainly to the constant dimness of the colouring, which may well have been a matter of deliberate choice and can certainly not be explained merely as a result of some unsuccessful technical experiment, of bad preservation. On the other hand, he allows hard, pointed lights to dart out from the twilit atmosphere of the background, and these set off figures which move in a peculiar wavering manner, making uncanny, and even obscene gestures. In the upper row the god Vulcan, on a car drawn by and full of apes, is the very caricature of a god—a skinny puppet with repulsively feminine lines.[81] With a long claw-like finger this being points to itself. In the cave on the left the one-eyed cyclopes are forging the weapons of Mars with curiously unsuitable, dancing movements, while on the right Mars himself and Venus betray the triumphant husband. A crowd of ugly Erotes grin at the shameless scene. The nonchalance with which the clothes and weapons of which the pair of lovers have divested themselves are spread out in front of their couch lends an ironical, challenging note to the scene. The 'picture within a picture' to the left of the cave, where we see the she-wolf with Romulus and Remus before the silhouette of the city of Rome, seems to be stuck on to the rest and is a pictorial jest known to the painters of antique murals and indefatigably copied by miniaturists.

In the frieze of the middle row, in the middle compartment, a severed hand emerges in a ghostly manner from the blue of the ground, holding the zodiacal sign of the Balance. Above and on either side are decan divinities. On the left, the nineteenth decan, an elegantly attired page of the Court, who with puffed-out 40 cheeks and an absurd threatening mien is blowing a trumpet—an iconological attribute of 'Vainglory'. In his free right hand he holds, as well as his lance, the 'inverted bird' prescribed by the old decan lists.[78] As conceived by Tura, this bird is the boaster's 'bag', and the victorious blast on his trumpet forms an absurd contrast to the pettiness of his achievement. This is obviously a derisive characterization of a 'swollen-headed enemy'. In the right-hand compartment a heavily armed archer is threatening an unarmed, naked man, who wrings his hands in 41 despair. This is the twenty-first decan of astrological pictorial tradition,[78] and Tura turns it into a dramatic study of mood with a moralizing significance: he incorporates it with characteristics such as 'violence' and 'thoughtless unreadiness'. The twentieth decan crouching in the middle above the scales should, according to Apomasar and Varahamihira, either 'fly' or 'fall'.[78] Here, however, he raises his arms to the same height as those of the balance at his feet, and his face and hands are turned towards the sky. In these gestures, in the despairing glance and in the half-open mouth we have a striking expression of that 'hunger and thirst' which Varahamihira required for this astrological demon. Is it a 'hunger and thirst' for justice, of which the balance is the symbol? If we consider the significance of the picture as a whole, we may perhaps perceive here a special, political allusion: in the loggia on the left important diplomatic negotiations are taking place; the atmosphere is filled with the watchful reserve of the participants, Borso weighs the words he speaks to his adversary, the ambassador, who to judge by his attire is a Venetian.[80] Even the usual hunting cortège on the right here lacks its normal cheerfulness and harmlessness, and it would seem as if Tura wanted to illustrate the jest handed down by several chroniclers, that Duke Borso conquered more territory during his hunting expeditions than others did by means of wars. In all this Tura was probably thinking of the tension between Ferrara and Venice, which ten years later was to result in a war involving Ferrara in many dangers.[80] The panegyrical theme of the *September*—Borso, the vigilant statesman—found through Tura a pictorial form which is individually and wittily 'deliberate', and at the same time profound and convincing.

Together with the little Washington *Madonna,* the Schifanoia frescoes are, 32 among the works of Tura that have been preserved, the extreme example of the angular style. This style dominates almost the whole of the paintings in the hall and its decorative efficacy is here strikingly affirmed. All idea of form seems to have been compressed into those wilful vertical, horizontal and diagonal lines first 28–33 seen in the St. Maurelius tondi and in the *Madonna.* This gives the pictures a clear, taut appearance, firm despite all the movement they contain. With their hard, pointed breaks, or their precise joints, these lines form triangular or quadrangular geometrical figures; they are concentrated so as to form compact ornaments which are the determining element of all decoration. Tura's style of fresco-painting, of which we have no other example, must, to judge from what preceded and followed, have achieved about 1470 the particular nuance that we see in the Schifanoia frescoes.

If Tura was the leading master in the Hall of the Months, then he must have provided his assistants and collaborators with a plentiful supply of sketches, as well as compositional schemes and cartoons, such as were actually used in this case, as can be seen from the numerous dotted lines that are still visible. In the will which he made in 1471—the year in which the frescoes were completed—mention is made of a large stock of drawings which the master wished to bequeath to a pupil or colleague named Domenico.[82] In the Albertina in Vienna there is a drawing of VIA two Turks, very Tura-esque, though it has been considerably retouched, which in subject and style is very close to the frescoes. It should be compared with the group VIB of Orientals on the left in the upper row of the *June,* by Cicognara. Akin to the Vienna drawing is another in Milan, showing a group of knights, which recurs in a similar form in practically all the 'loggia scenes' in Palazzo Schifanoia. One cannot, however, claim more for these drawings than that they were in some way connected with those designs of Tura which were used in Palazzo Schifanoia, as were numerous sketches for similar designs to be seen in Marco Zoppo's sketchbook, now in the British Museum in London.[83]

The contemporaneous decorations in the chapel at Belriguardo, probably a free-standing separate domed building, consisted only in part of paintings. They were for the most part stucco reliefs with all kinds of ornaments and rows of angels; Tura himself worked here as an architectural sculptor, together with two unnamed assistants. To form an idea of Tura's style in this field, we must turn once more to 14, 15 his paintings, which provide us with many hints. In particular we must study the 32, 44, 61 artistically decorated thrones of his goddesses and saints, the pillars, ceilings and IIIA, 25–7 walls in the paintings on the organ door, in the Schifanoia frescoes and in the 53 Roverella altar-piece, the richly adorned spandrels and friezes with which he embellished his painted buildings. All of these reveal great skill in architectural sculpture and a subtle execution, as well as a boldness, one might even say an audacity, of invention. We can well believe that the stucco reliefs at Belriguardo were just as audacious and imaginative. Tura and his assistants painted and gilded them in the most sumptuous manner.

There was very little real painting—fresco or *'secco ad olio'*, as was stipulated in the contract. Beneath the main dome Tura executed eight half-lengths of Evangelists and Fathers of the Church in semicircular fields, in the small dome of the lantern a God the Father. On 31 March 1472, a written valuation of the work, listing all the details, was made by Baldassare d'Este and Antonio Orsini, the latter having been proposed by Tura himself. This work has been completely lost. According to Venturi, there is one (doubtful) relic of the paintings in the dome— the sketch in Bayonne of a Father (or Doctor) of the Church lecturing.[84] Xc

VI

In 1471, the year in which the works in Palazzo Schifanoia and Belriguardo were completed, Duke Borso died, and his younger brother Ercole ascended the throne. In 1472–3 Tura again made designs for craftsmen and other odd jobs, mainly on the occasion of the preparations for the wedding of the duke. About the same time he entered upon a new period of activity as a Court portraitist, starting with portraits of the duke and his daughter Lucrezia. In their main lines these were similar to the portrait of a prince painted in the early 1450's, but they were also looser and freer and no longer reveal the subtle attention to detail. We can form an idea of the portrait of Ercole, who had previously been painted by Baldassare d'Este, for about the same time a whole series of profile portraits of the duke in bust-length was made, resembling one another to such an extent that Tura's version can hardly have formed an exception in its essential features. From the year 1472 we have three portraits for medals and a relief in London made by Baldassare d'Este, who had been employed at the Ferrarese Court as a specialist in portraiture since 1469; of somewhat later date are the portraits by Corradino da Modena[85] and Sperandio, the marble bust in Ferrara and the high relief in Paris, these last two being likewise the work of Sperandio.[86] Almost all these works show the same proudly raised profile with aquiline nose, the same protruding narrow-lipped mouth which is firmly closed, and the same long hair falling in strands from under the cap over the forehead and the nape of the neck; the breast is frequently covered with armour.

In 1472 Tura made designs for silverware. First he was commissioned to design a complete service of silver for the ducal table. This time the items in the chamberlain's register of payments give us more detailed information about the appearance of the pieces which the Venetian goldsmith Alegretto da Ragusa was commissioned to execute after Tura's designs. They consisted of thirty-six dishes of varying shape, purpose and size. They were ornamental and richly embellished with figures; satyrs, putti, griffins, dolphins, eagles, Estensian emblems, devices and crests, and foliage are mentioned as being among the ornamental motives. These ornaments were executed partly in niello, partly in painted enamel, relief and in the round, and we may imagine that they were as free in their movement, as lively, as imaginative and grotesque as they could possibly be. In all probability they were far removed from the sober conception of the ordinary household article they had to adorn; we have similar articles, of slightly later date, designed by the Paduan artist Andrea Riccio. Tura himself often introduced reproductions of goldsmith's work into his pictures and these show us his very individual taste in this field; 14 examples are the golden dolphins on the throne of the London *Venus,* the fantastic 21 headgear of the princess in the *St. George and the Dragon* in Ferrara, the costly jewels with which he adorns his goddesses and Madonnas. A very fanciful, delicately executed silver ship with a numerous crew in the treasury of Sant' Antonio at Padua is said to be derived from one of Tura's designs.[87] We are also told that the Este service pleased Lodovico il Moro so much that he wanted to have a similar one, to which end he frequently asked for Tura's drawings and apparently received them.[88]

From this period of particularly intensive work in the craftsman's field also date the only tapestries after Tura's designs that have been preserved and the only work of sculpture that Tura executed with his own hands.

The tapestries are pictorial and were probably intended for use in churches. The composition of both of them is the same, but they differ from one another in certain details, in their dimensions and also in quality. The tapestry in Cologne is IIIc the better of the two and is derived directly from Tura's cartoon; the version in IIc Cleveland was obviously copied from that in Cologne.[89]

The very compact, almost crowded composition consists of a number of kneeling figures, with one figure lying prone. Echoes of elements of the angular style are found in the drawing, but already seem to have been toned down. Instead of fanciful wit, we find expressive realism. The large heads on top of the heavy, thick-set bodies are most expressively ugly. Astounding is the inventiveness shown in the Herculean form of the body of Christ, stiff in death, with the sunken, dim eyes and the horribly distorted mouth; the body lies in the same attitude, with outstretched arms and bent knees, on the laps of the weeping women, as that in 49 which it hung on the cross. In the little *Crucifixion* by Tura in Cambridge, dating from the same period, we find this figure again.

46 The work of sculpture is a *Pietà,* formerly in a private collection in Florence. There is nothing in Emilian Sculpture of the second half of the Quattrocento that can be compared with it—only Tura's paintings. If we compare the Christ with

the Vienna *Pietà,* painted somewhat later, or the attitude of the Madonna with that 81
of the little picture of the *Virgin of the Annunciation* from the Consolazione altar- 9
piece in Rome, or the whole group with the *Pietà* at Venice, we can recognize 47
Tura's method of moulding forms, but the decisive factor is that this sculpture
possesses Tura's particular style of that time—suitably translated into sculpture.
The composition is of striking originality—there are no overlappings or inter-
weavings, the plastic limbs glide into delicate turns and bends, as if they were
afraid of being touched. Even the hands, raised in mourning, of the Mother with
the mighty head of a Sibyl, pause before they are folded. The compactness of the
group is achieved, not by means of connecting links, but by means of analogies.
This method of composition so characteristic of Tura can nowhere be better
appreciated than in this little work, in which those things become concretely perceptible which can only be hinted at in a painted picture owing to the fact that we
view it from one side only.[90] In the carefree, very personal 'calligraphy' of the
execution, the nearest approach to this work in terracotta is the pen drawing of a
Doctor of the Church teaching, in Bayonne, which Venturi brings into relation- Xc
ship with the half-lengths of Fathers of the Church in the dome at Belriguardo,
though more recently Tura's authorship has been denied. There is much to be said
for the alternative attribution to Giovanni Bellini,[91] for against the attribution to
Tura there is the all too free and indefinite calligraphy. Noteworthy, on the other
hand, are certain characteristic details such as the hand holding the book, with its
curiously bent thumb, a motive almost exactly repeated in Tura's drawing of a 71
man reading in Florence; and also the hanging cloth, which we have already seen
in the Milan *Charity*, in the Bergamo *Madonna* and in other works by Tura. And V, 80
lastly, the arrangement of the tubular folds hung like garlands over the ground, a
last echo of that 'angular style' which frequently recurs during this period.

A drawing the authenticity of which cannot be disputed is the design for an
altar-piece (apparently a small one) in London.[92] The subject is a Madonna 44
enthroned with the Child eating cherries and two Saints standing on either side: on
the left, St. Sebastian and St. Francis, on the right, St. Dominic and St. Agatha. The
St. Francis is very similar to the figure of the same Saint on the little household
altar made for Ercole I and now in Washington, while the St. Dominic is found 66
again in the later St. Dominic panel in Florence. In the motives of the nibbling 77
Child and the Saints standing steeply erect by the side of the Madonna, the composition is a distant reminder of the chief panel of the Consolazione altar-piece, 12
but everything has become more restrained, and tranquil. While the tapestries of the
Lamentation and the *Pietà* in terracotta still revealed a seeking after unusual ideas IIc, IIIc, 47
and effects, such as those which dominated the early period of Tura's maturity, we

now perceive that Tura is at the same time striving to return to traditional forms. The process begins with this drawing. The wainscoting of the wall was to have a gold ground and the artist has written the word 'Horo' (gold) eleven times in the respective panels. The surrounds of these panels look like picture-frames round the figures of the Saints in front of them. It seems as if Tura were playing with the idea of returning from the scheme of one large main panel, in which the figures taking part in the *Sacra Conversazione* are combined on one plane in one room, to the long-since discarded layout of a polyptych, for the five figures stand side by side but isolated from one another, as if they were waiting to be separated by frames. As a matter of fact, in his later works, Tura showed a preference for polyptychs.

The sharp tenseness of the Schifanoia period is no longer discernible in the folds, which are more tranquil and at the same time looser; they are just as detached from the ground and just as 'garland-like' in the way they hang over the limbs, as Xc they are in the Bayonne drawing. In the linear ductus the melodic element begins to supplant the rhythmical, and the calligraphy becomes soft and tender. The bodies become fuller, and in the forms, attitudes and gestures display a kind of comfortable majesty.

We find these tendencies again in a number of small religious paintings dating from the early 1470's. First, in the curious *St. John on the island of Patmos,* in 45 Genoa.[93] The sturdy Saint is lying in an old-fashioned attitude, almost as if he had been poured out of a mould. Everything is infinitely tranquil; not a human being is to be seen in the desert landscape—a strange vision of an Arizona prairie with towering rocks—in which the prevailing elements are silence and the remoteness and immobility of time come to a standstill.

49   The *Crucifixion* at Cambridge is, in its composition, of extreme simplicity, symmetry and firmness.[94] The mourning gestures of the two figures beneath the Cross are sweeping and heavy, and full of significance. It seems as if Tura had drawn his inspiration for this picture from works of sculpture, perhaps the Crucifixion group, similar in its arrangement, by Nicolò and Giovanni Baroncelli and Domenico di Paris, in the cathedral at Ferrara.

47   The *Pietà* in Venice, highly esteemed by Tura's contemporaries, inevitably reflected the particular mood of this period of his development.[95] The motive and composition of the Madonna, who is seated and holds her dead Son upon her knees, are derived from centuries of tradition. Here Tura seems to be following every detail of the mediaeval vesperal pictures and to be deliberately trying to be 'old-fashioned'. The dead Christ is far too small in proportion to the weeping Mother and is as pitiably ugly as the carved figures of northern Late Gothic. But the interpretation, individual in every respect, of the traditional theme is

unmistakably that of Tura and his Ferrarese milieu; the conventional pathos of the lament for the dead is replaced by a courtly gesture—the Mother, her eyes averted in a peculiar way, raises the hand of the dead Christ to her mouth, in order to kiss it reverently. In the orange tree to the left the symbolical ape is crouching like a ghost, and this raises the scene above the narrow limits of its actual significance, calling upon the pious spectator to follow in the footsteps of Christ.

This picture repeats in its main features the composition of the *Crucifixion* in 49 Cambridge—complete, classical symmetry of construction, consisting of a broad horizontal scheme with a steeply-rising vertical in the centre, the simplest form of composition imaginable. The brushwork has a delicate tenderness and compactness and the colouring is Venetian in its fullness and warmth. If the characters on the sarcophagus represent, as is believed, the enciphered form, adorned with flourishes, of Tura's signature, then we can also deduce from the ornamentation in the second panel from the right the date of the picture, 1472—a date which agrees with what can be deduced from the style.

In any case, to judge by the stage of development, this little *Pietà* comes immediately before the large *Roverella altar-piece*, which can be dated 1474, the year 50–9 of Bishop Lorenzo Roverella's death, an event mentioned in the inscription, partially revealed as a result of restoration, on the little organ stool in the centre panel 56 in London.[96] The various portions of the triptych, including a semi-circular lunette and the predella, have for the most part been preserved, but are now very scattered. Its original form and the various objects represented were recorded by Baruffaldi,[97] who saw it before it had been badly damaged during the siege of 1709, in its original location in the church of San Giorgio, on a wall in front of the Maurelius chapel already containing an altar-piece by Tura.[98] In addition to this, we can form an idea of it from the numerous works of the same kind to which Tura's painting must have formed a parallel as regards composition and arrangement. Of these the most important are Mantegna's altar-piece in San Zeno, Verona (1456–9); Francesco Benaglio's altar-piece of San Bernardino in the same city (1462); Giorgio Schiavone's triptych in the cathedral at Padua (about 1460, centre panel in Berlin); the two triptychs by Bartolomeo Vivarini (1474 and 1482) and that by Giovanni Bellini in the Frari at Venice (1488).

In its dimensions also, if we remember that it must certainly have had at one time an elaborate framework, Tura's triptych corresponds with Mantegna's San Zeno altar-piece (which measures 189 by 177 inches). It had, however, more compartments; the middle panel was more than 30 inches higher than the wings, though above the latter there were two other panels containing figures in half-length. The lunette was higher than in Mantegna's altar-piece and contained figures. Apart from these differences, it cannot be denied that in this work Tura followed Mantegna more closely than ever before. In the centre panel of the

50 London altar-piece, as in that of San Zeno, the Madonna is sitting high up on her throne, surrounded by a group of angel musicians, in an open Renaissance hall, which is continued logically on the wings. On these are monumentally conceived figures of Saints, standing one behind the other in echelon formation running into depth. The difference is that in Tura's more compact and at the same time simpler composition the effect of an echelon running into depth is partially nullified by the fact that in each of the spatial triangles in front there is one kneeling figure, whereas in Mantegna's altar-piece these spaces are empty—in front of St. Paul and St.

51 Maurelius on the right wing (now in Rome) kneels the General of the Olivetans, Nicolò Roverella,[99] while according to Baruffaldi, on the left wing (now lost

52 except for the head of the St. George), the deceased bishop Lorenzo Roverella was shown kneeling in front of St. Peter and St. George. The bishop was shown in the act of knocking (on the gateway to Paradise), an appropriate illustration of the words in the inscription on the organ in the centre panel: 'Surge puer: Roverella fores gens pultat. apertum redde aditum' etc.[100]

The half-length figures above the wings were those of St. Benedict and St. Bernard, and scenes from the legends of these saints formed the subjects of the predella panels. All these portions have been lost, but the lunette has been pre-

57 served and is now in Paris; it contains a *Lamentation* with numerous figures. Roberto Longhi has made an enlightening reconstruction of the Roverella altar-piece, the only doubtful point in which is the predella, described by him as containing other subjects than those mentioned by Baruffaldi.[101]

A typical example of this stage in Tura's development, aiming at greater tranquillity and firmness, the Roverella altar-piece is the most 'classical', the most cheerful and vigorous, and also the least complicated work that he painted. It is sumptuous in its colouring, perfectly symmetrical in its composition, broad and firm in its painting technique. The figures are for the most part solid and robust, their gestures and attitudes tranquil and dignified, the expression of the countenances well balanced, and, in the case of the male personages, often energetic. These saints stand firmly and compactly on the well-constructed pictorial plane.

51 The St. Paul would seem to have been influenced by Pizzolo's version of this Saint in the Ovetari Chapel and by Mantegna's in the San Zeno altar-piece, but the effect in Tura's picture is more virile and worldly, an astonishing fact in a work by the esoteric Tura.

The linear rhythm has a slow-gliding, ponderously swinging character. The full limbs stand out from the draperies as broad curved surfaces, the folds radiating from them have again become—after the 'naturalistic' intermezzo of the early 1470's—a trifle more ornamental and they form rounded, spiral-shaped figures; particularly noteworthy is the run of the folds on the left arm of the St. Paul and on the legs of the Madonna. Only the *Lamentation* in the lunette at the Louvre, 57 filled with ecstatic, rather theatrical movement, forms an exception to the general tranquillity; in any case, it fulfils that need of 'contrast', to which Tura even in this painting had to remain faithful. To obtain a proper idea of the beauties of the *Lamentation* and of the whole of the Roverella altar-piece, one must examine from close at hand all the details in which Tura's whole power of expression is concentrated.

A balanced mood, tranquillity in the midst of movement, broadness of line in the draughtsmanship and modelling, are to be found in several smaller works, all of which have been deemed to form part of the Roverella altar-piece, but probably have nothing to do with it, except that they were painted about the same time. These are four little panels of an *Annunciation with two Saints* (all the figures are standing) in Washington[101] and three charming little narrative panels containing 64–7 scenes from the childhood of Christ with many figures in Cambridge, Boston and New York.[102] The former are probably connected with a little altar carved by 60–3 Bernardino da Venezia, which was presented to Duke Ercole I and which he commissioned the goldsmith Amadio da Milano[103] to embellish with niello inlays, while Cosimo Tura executed the paintings for it. The centre panel contained a Madonna and Child, and on the inside and outside of the wings are four figures of Saints. The figure of the Bishop Saint on the right was inspired by the statue of St. Maurelius in Baroncelli's bronze *Crucifixion* in the cathedral at Ferrara.[104]

About the middle of the 1470's Tura also executed several series of designs for craftsmen and towards the end of the decade he painted a few portraits. One of these, the portrait of the one-year-old Prince Alfonso, painted in 1477, seems to have been so successful that Tura had later to paint two repetitions of it. There is a medal dating from the same year by an unknown master (Hill 118), on which the little Alfonso is shown in bust length in profile, and this was probably based on Tura's successful portrait. Another portrait, executed in 1479, showed Lucrezia d'Este in bust length and was a return gift for the portrait of the young Annibale Bentivoglio presented to the Ferrarese Court in the previous year.

In 1477 Tura was again commissioned to execute a series of Allegories for an unspecified 'studio' of Duke Ercole—allegedly Belfiore.[105] As to the subject-matter of the series, we know only that it was to contain seven 'nude women'. Only three of these had to be entirely new, since four already existed and had merely to be altered. We have already mentioned above that the existing paintings

were in all probability earlier works by Tura himself, that the Berlin drawing
13 of *Charity* dating from the 1460's was probably a preliminary study for one of
them and that the seven 'nude women' of 1477–81 may have been a series of
cardinal virtues (nudity in this case being understood as symbolizing purity and
sincerity). We have several examples of Tura's attitude towards the nude during
the 1470's—for the most part male nudes. Among these the body of the Christ in
47 the Venice *Pietà* must be considered a 'Gothic' exception, repeated in a much
57 milder form in the *Lamentation* of the Roverella altar-piece. In general, Tura's
nudes at this time had a certain softness and fullness—for example, the *St. Sebas-*
44, 49 *tian* in the London sketch for an altar-piece and the *Crucified Christ* in Cambridge. The *Hercules* in Rotterdam, dating from the same period as the 'nude
70 women', is as florid as one of Michelangelo's nudes—an effect to which the broad
calligraphy of the brush-work contributes. This *Hercules* would appear to have
been a study for an allegory having some connection with Duke Ercole.

13   Female nudes are less frequent in Tura's work and they are invariably pleasing,
27 somewhat muscular figures of young girls. The finest are the reliefs of Juno, Luna
25 and Venus on the walls of the *Annunciation* on the organ door and the St.
44 Agatha in the sketch for an altar-piece in London.

Something of the florid strength of the Hercules is found, curiously enough, in
69 the half-length nude figure of *St. Jerome doing penance*, in London. Tura has
refrained from giving this figure any perceptible tokens of asceticism and has
deliberately concentrated all the expression of ardent devotion aroused by the
appearance of the Crucified Christ in the passionately upturned eyes of the Saint.
Unfortunately the work is a fragment; in the Certosa at Ferrara it formed part of
a large and important altar-piece, which was later dispersed. Another fragment
of the same altar-piece is the little figure of Christ, in the attitude of the Crucified
68 Christ, floating down from the sky, now in the Brera in Milan.[106] If we arrange
the two fragments properly, we see that in the London fragment large portions
are missing at the top and on the right, and that the original altar-piece must have
been one and a half times as high and twice as wide. The impression which the
original must have produced has been falsified by the cutting—there was once a
spacious landscape in which the figure of the saintly penitent must have looked
more forlorn and less monumental than it does in the fragment.

In its colouring the picture has a fascinating harmony: silvery yellow tones in
the gentlest nuances dominate the whole, and the pure reds of the cardinal's hat and
a book stand out like delicate accents from the greenish-brown ground on which
they lie. Stylistically the figure of the St. Jerome is still close to the Roverella altar-
piece and it must therefore date from the second half of the 1470's.

In 1480 Tura painted another portrait to the duke's order, that of his daughter Isabella, a gift to her betrothed, Francesco Gonzaga. He also made designs for tapestries, one of these being that which was woven by Rubinetto, the only tapestry with figures which the sources mention as having been designed by Tura. The subject of this lost work was the 'Story of Solomon'—either the Judgement of Solomon or the visit of the Queen of Sheba. In 1481 he collaborated with an intarsia-worker named Tasto Tortoletto.[107]

From the last decade of Tura's activity only religious works have been preserved, and we know of only one profane work—a bust-length portrait, painted in 1485, of Beatrice d'Este, the bride of Lodovico il Moro. This was the only work executed by Tura for the Court between 1480 and his death in 1495. About 1480 the ageing and lonely artist painted several polyptychs according to old-fashioned customary notions, which must obviously all have been of the same construction and even of the same format. A number of almost identical paintings all of the same size, with semicircular tops, mostly representing Saints standing erect against a gold ground, have been preserved in various places. Attempts have been made 72–80 to assemble all or some of these to form an altar-piece, such as that vaguely described by contemporaries as having been executed by Tura for the church of San Luca at Borgo, Ferrara.[108]

In style, colouring and technique, as well as in certain compositional details, there are, however, differences which practically exclude the possibility of combining the nine panels in question to form one polyptych. Moreover there are two panels with enthroned personages, which must have been the centre panels of two different altar-pieces. And lastly, we know from the statements of chroniclers that there existed three (if not more) polyptychs by Tura with single panels of Saints against a gold ground, specifically described as being similar in composition and construction: in San Luca in Borgo, Ferrara, in San Romano near the cathedral, and in the church of San Giacomo in Argenta.[109]

If we take into consideration all the historical and stylistic factors, and those of composition and content, the nine surviving panels can be assigned to three clearly delineated groups forming parts of three separate polyptychs. Format and composition tell us fairly clearly that these five-panel altar-pieces were of the kind of which we have numerous examples by Bartolomeo Vivarini, Carlo Crivelli and other painters.

It is difficult to say from which of the three churches mentioned, or other churches, the three altar-pieces of which fragments have been preserved originally came. There is only a certain probability that the group of panels to which the *Madonna* in Bergamo belongs formed with other parts, since lost, the altar-piece 80 in San Giacomo, since C. Cittadella states that there was a painting of the Madonna in that church.

The provenance of the three altar-pieces is uncertain, but the dates of execution are easily established. Although they differ from one another in stylistic nuances, they are all close to the last work by Tura of which the date is known for certain—

83 the large *St. Anthony of Padua* in the Galleria Estense at Modena, painted in 1484.[110] This is also the date assigned by indirect tradition to the San Luca altar-piece[111] and there is every probability that it might be applicable to our Polyptych B. In many respects Polyptych A has points in common with earlier works by Tura; Polyptych C, on the other hand, is very close to the *St. Anthony* of 1484 in its degree of stylistic development.

72, 74   The surviving panels of Polyptych A—the *St. Christopher* and the *St. Sebastian* in Berlin—are distinguished from the others by an unusually open, almost sketch-like brushwork, by the warm, brownish modelling and by the temperamental unruliness of the spiritual expression. In addition to this, these two Saints, unlike the others, are standing in an open landscape and the proportions of their bodies are notably smaller.

In the *St. Sebastian*, we can see how that tendency towards a firmer delineation of forms is now leading to the rigidity which becomes ever greater in Tura's last period. This nude, in the attitude reminiscent of the Master of Flémalle, and the overstressed anatomy recalling Mantegna, produces a stiff, old-fashioned effect. We
28, 29   are reminded once again of the doll-like warriors in the St. Maurelius tondi dating from the end of the 1460's, but the stiff, tight-drawn loincloth of the Saint no longer has any trace of the bold manner of the 'angular' style, while the fluttering
72   robe of the *St. Christopher* does not seem to be really in movement, but only ornamentally arranged.

All the feeling is again concentrated in the heads. The fervour of Sebastian's
73   upturned gaze, the suffering in Christopher's twisted features are fascinatingly unequivocal examples of psychological expression.

71   The brush drawing, painted rather than drawn, of a *Man reading* in Florence shows how Tura tentatively evolved drapery folds of the most unusual type found
75   in the *St. James enthroned* at Caen, the centre panel of Polyptych B. The realism of the model is transmuted into ornamentality, the 'formula' begins to appear, afterwards to be fulfilled in the painting. The customary early dating of this drawing and the alleged relationship to the lost frescoed figures at Belriguardo seem hardly probable; this is not Tura's manner around 1470, but his last manner, that of about 1480.

75–7   The three surviving panels of Polyptych B blend with one another in the heightened smoothness of the painting, in the calligraphic regularity of the hatched 'writing', in an increasing abstraction of the co-ordinating details, and in the harmony of the spiritual concentration. (In addition to these, there are certain external elements, such as the fact that the figures are seen slightly from below and the haloes are similarly treated.) Stylistically, the most clearly defined is the *St. James* 75 in Caen. The play of the folds, regularly hatched, produces the effect of an artistic construction without any characterization of the actual material; a truly manneristic system of lines in reality is nothing but an ear-shell ornament. 'Nature' and the power of persuasion through the senses are sacrificed to a dramatic melodiousness, the tense notes of which we enjoy without demanding any concrete relationship to the subject or its essence.

The expression of the sickly, ugly boy's face of this St. James does not reproduce the characteristics of a certain saintly personage, but is an interpretation of the particular spiritual condition of one who is destined to be called. There are various nuances here, which Tura renders with a subtle differentiation: in contrast to the ecstasy of St. James, the silent absorption of the St. Anthony, the gentle awe of 76 St. Dominic, whose hands joined in prayer hardly touch each other and extend 77 with a protective gesture above an invisible treasure. Tura's pietism oversteps the bounds of the usual and the popularly accepted to such an extent that it attains an almost fantastic grandeur.

In the *St. James* altar-piece there are probably reminiscences of Mantegna; in its arrangement and internal measurements it corresponds with the latter's altarpiece of *St. Luke* in Milan (1453–4), though we do not know whether Tura's Polyptych also contained a second, upper row of half-figures.

The centre panel (now cut on all sides) of Polyptych C was the *Madonna* in 78–82 Bergamo; the so-called *St. Louis* in New York and the *St. Nicholas of Bari* or *St. Barnabas* in Nantes were two of the originally four side-panels. The lunette was probably the (now much shortened) painting of *Two Angels supporting the dead Christ*, in Vienna.[112] All four panels have the same notably smooth brushwork and differ from both the other groups; the *Madonna* and the *St. Louis* show the greatest similarity in the remarkably jagged style of the folds. That the two Saints belong to the same picture is proved by the identical way in which the folds of the exaggeratedly long robes are twisted and piled up on the ground. Something similar to this can be seen in the Angel of the Annunciation in the little altar-piece 64 of 1475, where it had a certain vivacious elegance; it is found again in the *St. Anthony* of 1484 at Modena, but in this case the folds dragging on the ground grip 83 the feet of the figure like a vice. In contrast to the figures of the two other groups, these Saints are seen slightly from below, as is also the group of the *Lamentation* in the lunette. Everything coincides so exactly that it is permissible to assume that the four panels once formed part of the same altar-piece.

79   The 'ornamental' manner is found in its most extreme form in the *St. Nicholas,* in which the folds of the robe fall in even waves. The abstractness has the expressiveness of a psychogram and expresses the artist rather than the person repre-
80 sented. The head of the Madonna, with the lofty white forehead and the large eyes protruding from under sunken eyelids, looks like a religious mask made of porcelain. This unapproachable Mother of God, surrounded by cold air, infinitely distant and pure, is one of those human forms painted by Tura which have no human foundation whatever. Tura clothes his conception of a 'perfectness' surpassing all experience in the complete harmony of lines and curves intertwining in accordance with a regular pattern with a smoothness and regularity elaborated to the last degree, which makes the picture seem like the work of a mechanic rather than of a craftsman.

The colouring has a peculiar sharpness. The cold blue and madder red of the clothing and the bluish-white of the flesh form blend so well with the gold of the ground that the picture simply cannot be compared even with the more coherent works of other masters, however high their quality, for each would disturb the other. Tura's art, based on arrangement, stands absolutely alone, since it is as far from the classical solution as it is from the sensational audacities of pioneers. The sharp colouring of the *Madonna* is in harmony with the iciness of the tones in the
81 Vienna *Pietà,* dominated by the landscape background with its bluish, violet and greenish nuances, the blues and reds of the Angels' robes, the glittering white of the dead body of Christ. Everything seems to be made of the same congealed material—the rigid, motionless folds of the draperies, the gleaming, smooth bodies
opp. p. 14 and faces, the transparent figures of the three Marys in the background, which have not been separately treated, but are lightly sketched in with the point of the brush against the landscape and the sky.

The artistic tendencies revealed in the three polyptychs are combined and ful-
83 filled in the altar-piece with the monumental single figure of *St. Anthony of Padua,* now in the Galleria Estense at Modena, painted, as we know from one of Tura's letters, in 1484.[113]

This picture, too, has been cut, reduced considerably in size and deprived of important portions, so that today it produces a false impression. According to C. Cittadella, the original altar-piece was in the church of San Nicolò and was particularly noteworthy on account of a 'nobile architettura' in which the figure of the Saint stood.[114] Of this only a narrow edge has remained, of a delicate madder-red colour, but this exquisitely coloured frame must originally have been far larger and more impressive. In the form of what is left and in the size of the figure, the *St. Anthony* resembles a monumental *St. Jerome* in the Pinacoteca at Ferrara, probably an early work by Ercole Roberti.[115] If the latter picture was really inspired by Tura's *St. Anthony*, the panel in Modena had probably the same proportions and must have been half as high and half as wide.

In its 'abstractness' and rigidity the *St. Anthony* surpasses even the *St. James* in Caen and the *St. Nicholas* in Nantes. The powerful body of the Saint is like a 75, 79 statue carved in stone, the limbs appear to move mechanically on socket-joints, or at least that is the effect produced by the left knee, which protrudes beneath the material of the cowl. In places—for example, above the left thigh and beneath the knee—the folds have no motive at all; they form petrified straight lines, angles, ellipses and spirals. The brushwork is very smooth and subtly finished. Nowhere, however, do these characteristics produce an effect of weakness. The bold and deliberate exaggeration with which they are presented, constitute the grandeur of this incomparable achievement. This last work by Cosimo Tura that has been preserved is, in fact, one of his most striking productions. The effect of inconsolable grief and fading gentleness in this classical picture of a monk is due mainly 84 to the colouring. The warm colour of the face and the creamy white of the cowl stand out like stars against the misty sky, which passes from dark blue through gentle nuances to the gorgeous fireworks of a yellow and red sunset over the sea. On the surface of the water, broken by little silvery waves, the colour-scheme is 85 mirrored, so that the lower part of the background ends with the same velvety, melancholy blue with which it began at the top. Above the lightest portion, where sky and water meet, is the lightest portion of the figure, which here seems to dissolve in light. (Such expressive lighting effects reappeared thirty years later, burning brighter, in the work of Grünewald.)

So far as we know, this *St. Anthony* painted in 1484 was Tura's last work. We are told that one year later he was commissioned to paint a portrait. Evidently he was working very little at the time. The few pictures which, almost immediately after beginning them, he left to others to complete, such as the *Virgin of the Annunciation* in the National Gallery, London, or the *Portrait of an Old Man* in IV the Museo Poldi-Pezzoli, Milan, probably date from these last years. In trifles such XIIIA as the woodcut illustration for 'Alfraganus' (see Chronological List, page 84, No. 67)—it is a significant fact that this was an astronomical work—we seem to meet once again in 1493 Tura the designer of all kinds of articles for everyday use. In 1487 he made his second will; in 1491, his third, during a long illness. Four years later, at the age of sixty-five, Cosimo Tura died.

VII

At the height of his fame Tura had numerous pupils, assistants and imitators. Nevertheless we do not know for certain, and it is difficult to believe, that he had a workshop in the proper sense of the word. In the works that have come down to us we find no trace of that harmonious agreement, that flawless dovetailing of the artist's own work and that of his pupils, which is normally found during the Middle Ages and also during the Renaissance. Tura's works are either completely his own down to the last detail and easily recognizable as such, or else they are his own only as regards certain portions which can be clearly defined and to which the portions executed by assistants offer a sharp contrast. Examples of the latter category are the Schifanoia frescoes and the *Allegories of Virtues* in Milan and

V, XIIb Florence. On the other hand there are only a few doubtful cases: pictures partly in Tura's manner, but, taken as a whole, too weak in quality, and showing too little originality, to permit of their being attributed unreservedly to him. Such

IV pictures are the fragment of a *Virgin of the Annunciation* in London,[116] a portrait
XIIIa of an old man in Milan,[117] which at the very most can only have been started by
XIb the master.[118] The little half-length *Madonna* from the Paolini collection[119] is certainly an imitation or a copy, made without Tura ever setting eyes on it, and the same can be said of the repetition of Tura's Venice *Pietà*, in Chicago.[120]

Tura employed assistants only from time to time, when he had large-scale commissions to execute, and he changed them constantly. About 1460 he probably

XVI worked in collaboration with the much older Michele Pannonio. In 1461 he had an assistant named Bartolomeo, presumably Bartolomeo Rosetti of Modena, whom we frequently hear of in Ferrara. In the same year Giangaleazzo Sforza sent a young artist to Tura to work with him as an apprentice. During the decoration of the chapel in the castle of Belriguardo Tura had two assistants, whose names are not specified. In Palazzo Schifanoia his collaborators and assistants were Francesco del Cossa, Baldassare d'Este and Antonio Cicognara. In his will made in 1471, Tura bequeaths to an artist (probably one of his pupils) named Domenico all his drawings and his working equipment. In 1482 he engaged a certain Antonio as his assistant; another assistant was Francesco Majoli.[121] Others who worked with him and under his instructions were the weavers, embroiderers, goldsmiths and silversmiths whose names have been mentioned; here too there is little trace of any continuous collaboration.

Almost all the miniaturists who worked in the Estensian territories during the reigns of Borso and Ercole I were influenced by Tura in a free and purely artistic

way. The most gifted among them were Guglielmo Giraldi del Magro and, perhaps, Franco de' Russi (provided the attribution to him of a large number of Xв
stylistically similar miniatures is correct). These artists are closer to Tura in conception, style, and also in quality, than any other painter influenced by him. Their
forms are generous and full, their calligraphy has a florid elasticity and manneristic
fluidity, expression and mood are deliberate and full of meaning. A more delicate,
more nervous and perhaps also more spirited ability is revealed in a number of
miniatures which make use of Tura's 'angular style' of the 1460's and often
repeat individual motives from his pictures or whole compositions. The most
gifted miniaturists of this school would seem to have been Jacopo Filippo d'Argenta XIA
and Fra Evangelista da Reggio, probably pupils of Giraldi.[122] Both of them, as
well as the miniaturist Martino da Modena, can be proved to have been in personal contact with Tura.

Antonio Cicognara, Tura's assistant in Palazzo Schifanoia, imitated the leading
master not only in several miniatures, but also in frescoes and in large and small
panel-paintings. After very provincial and crude, but already slightly manneristic
beginnings (a *Madonna* in the Pinacoteca at Ferrara, under the wrongly retouched
date 1480, which should be back-dated about fifteen years, a *St. Jerome in his study*
in the Accademia at Ravenna, and frescoes and ceiling paintings in the convent of
Sant' Antonio in Polesine), he took great pains to draw nearer to Cossa and Tura.
In Palazzo Schifanoia, where he did more of the work than any of the other artists, VIв, VIIв
he is nearer to Cossa. Later, in his more mature imitations of Tura, he produced his
best works: a *Madonna with the Child in a landscape* (Boston, Mass.), a large
Ascension full of figures in the abbey of Nonantola, and the little *Madonna
Enthroned*, close to Tura at least in its technique and colouring, in the Pinacoteca
at Bologna. Only about 1484 did he break away from the influence of Tura and
strive to achieve the softer style of Lorenzo Costa, as is proved by several small
paintings in Boston, Bergamo and Cremona, the stylistic tendencies of which are
subsequently combined in the signed and dated altar-piece showing the Madonna
enthroned between St. Agnes and St. Catherine, now in the Cologna collection,
Milan.[123] That Baldassare d'Este was also for some time under Tura's influence is XIIIв
shown by his fresco of horsemen on the north wall of the hall in Palazzo Schifanoia
and also by his little *St. George* in the Heinemann collection.[124]

Francesco del Cossa acknowledged the authority of the more famous Tura on
only one occasion, and that was in his *Prudentia* in Florence, which he painted
under Tura's supervision.[125] In Palazzo Schifanoia, on the other hand, Cossa's
own talent, equal to that of his master, already begins to assert itself. Ercole Roberti
is, in his sensitive spirituality, close to Tura, but he modelled his style on that of his IIIв

real master, Francesco del Cossa. A similar relationship existed in the case of another, extremely delicate painter of high quality, who worked in Faenza and has been identified (on doubtful grounds) as Leonardo Scaletti.[126] Lorenzo Costa, on the other hand, began by following Tura's style, and may even have worked in his studio; it is significant that what was probably his earliest picture, the *St. Sebastian* in Dresden, was still held to be by Tura even after Costa's signature written in Hebrew characters had long been deciphered.[127] According to the statements of contemporaries, there was once a triptych in the church of San Vito at Ferrara which the two artists painted in collaboration; the centre panel, a *Madonna*, was painted by Tura, and the side-panels, two *Fathers of the Church,* by Costa.[128] We may consider as due to experience gained in Tura's workshop the 'picture within a picture' to be seen in one of Lorenzo Costa's 'Trionfi' in the Bentivoglio chapel in San Giacomo Maggiore at Bologna (1488–90), the motive of the composition being the same as that found in Palazzo Schifanoia.

XIc

As is only natural, most of the imitations of Tura, and the most literal among them, are anonymous. A characteristic example is the beautiful half-length *Madonna* in Turin,[129] probably derived from the *Spes* in Florence which formed part of the cycle of Virtues painted under Tura's direction. Lastly, as a proof of the influence exercised by Tura on the production of household articles, mention must be made of a cabinet in Reggio, charmingly painted and partly in the style of Tura.[130]

XIIA
XIIB
IIB

It must, however, be admitted that this widespread influence of Tura on other, for the most part younger, artists, barely outlived the master, who before he died had to witness the gradual extinction of his own fame. Lorenzo Costa and Francesco Francia, who soon turned to other goals, attracted the younger generation towards their sentimental conceptions and their classical forms, striving to rival Raphael and to fulfil themselves in him. But the next step was taken by the important generation of 1500, the generation of Pontormo. These artists continued, probably without even thinking of the Quattrocento pioneers, what Squarcione had begun, and completed it. Emilian mannerists, and especially the most important among them, Parmigianino, were the real heirs and the brilliant corroborators of the timeless vital energy of Cosimo Tura's tense artistic conception.

NOTES TO THE INTRODUCTION

1. The year of birth was discovered by A. Venturi in a document dated 1430 (*Arch. Stor. dell'Arte*, 1894, p. 52); that of the artist's death by G. Campori ('I pittori degli Estensi', *Atti e Memorie etc. . . prov. Modenesi e Parm.*, 1885, p. 14: notes on the sources). According to Superbi (*Apparato de gli Hvomini Illustri*, Ferrara, 1620, p. 122), Tura died at the age of sixty-three.

2. Filarete, *Quellenschriften*, new series 3, p. 302. See also Venturi, 'Tura', *Preuss. Jahrb.*, 1888, p. 3; Giovanni Santi (and other Tura critics) in Padovani, *Critica d'arte e Pittura Ferrarese*, Rovigo, 1954, p. 41 f.

3. Most of the documents from which this and the following details concerning the life and work of Tura and the personages who formed his milieu are drawn have been published by L. N. Cittadella, *Ricordi e Documenti intorno alla vita di Cosimo Tura*, Ferrara, 1866, and *Notizie relative a Ferrara*, 1868, I, p. 569 f., II, especially pp. 108–80; see also G. Campori, *Pittori degli Estensi*, 1886; A. Venturi, article of 1888, and 'Documenti relative al Tura ecc.', in *Arch. Stor. dell'Arte*, 1894, p. 52 f.

4. The letter reproduced in facsimile in Venturi, *Preussisches Jahrbuch*, 1888, p. 31. Another, very faded and almost illegible letter of Tura's is, like this one, preserved in the Archivio di Stato, Modena, Busta C. T. Probably because they relied on Tura's second will, made in 1487, the place of burial is wrongly stated to be San Giorgio by M. A. Guarini (*Compendio Historico*, Ferrara, 1621, p. 393 f.) and G. A. Scalabrini (*Mem. Istor. delle Chiese di Ferrara*, Ferrara, 1773, Borghi, p. 29). Cf. Venturi, 1888, p. 32.

5. Giraldi, *Operum quae extant omnium*, II, Basle, 1580.

6. *Milanesi*, II, p. 142 f.

7. On Baruffaldi (1675–1755) see Padovani, *op. cit.*, pp. 95–115. The manuscripts of his *Vite de' Pittori e Scultori ferraresi* (printed in 1844) date from about 1702, 1710 and before 1735. The life of Tura was published separately in 1836.

8. *Pitture e Sculture di Ferrara*, Ferrara, 1770, p. 8. Cf. Dürer's sketches after the so-called 'Tarocchi of Mantegna', derived from Ferrarese models, and his drawings and engravings of Orpheus, likewise derived from a Ferrarese model (Hind, E III 17). Cf. A. Warburg, *Dürer und die italienische Antike* (1905), in *Gesammelte Schriften*, II, p. 445 f.; Meder, 'Neue Beiträge zur Dürer-Forschung', *Jahrb. d. AH. Kaiserhauses*, 1911, p. 213; H. Tietze and E. Tietze-Conrat, *Der junge Dürer*, Augsburg, 1928, pp. 13, 306 f.

9. Cesare Cittadella, *Catalogo Istorico dei Pittori e Scultori Ferraresi*, Ferrara, 1782–3, I, p. 48.

10. Payment for the painting of the organ door was made on 11 June 1469 (L. N. Cittadella, *Notizie relative a Ferrara*, 1868, I, p. 66). The contract for Belriguardo was signed on 30 May. The upper floor of Palazzo Schifanoia, which includes the Hall of the Months, was still being built in 1469 (Muratori, *Rer. Ital. Script.*, XXIV, col. 220); on 25 March 1470 Francesco Cossa announced that he had finished his share of the work (the east wall) (A. Venturi, 'Ein Brief des F. d. Cossa,' in *Der Kunstfreund*, 9, 1 May 1885). The painting of the Hall of the Months must thus have been commenced in 1469 and have been virtually finished in 1470. Additions to, and partial revisions of, the frescoes were made between April and August 1471 and from 1493.

11. The painting of the banner of the tailors' guild (1452) had to be modified in 1456. By order of Borso, Baldassare d'Este repainted in 1471 parts of the Schifanoia frescoes, which had only just been finished (cf. Note 10). In 1475 Tura had to repaint a little household altar, for the expressly stated reason that Duke Ercole did not like it. Between 1477 and 1481 Tura was asked by Duke Ercole to alter some already existing allegorical paintings, probably his own work, in the Duke's studio.

12. Designs for textiles were made in 1457, 1458, 1459, 1467, 1472, 1474, 1475 (?), 1479, 1480 and 1483 (?). Painting on articles made of cloth, leather, wood and metals in 1451, 1452, 1456, 1458–63, 1462, 1464, 1465.

Designs for goldsmith's work in 1473–4, and 1475 (?). Belriguardo, 1469–72; cf. Chronological List of Works and Note to Plate 46.

13. In Baruffaldi, *Vite*, I, p. 82. Cf. Reinhard Albrecht, 'T. V. Strozzi', *Programm des Königl. Gymnasiums Dresden*, Leipzig, 1891.

14. On the Madonna in Venice: SVIGLIA EL TUO FIGLIO DOLCE MADRE PIA PER FAR IN FIN FELICE LALMA MIA. On the Madonna in London: Surge puer. Rovorella fores gens pultat. apertum redde aditum. pulsa lex ait: intus eris. (Cf. M. Davies, *Nat. Gall. Cat.*, London, 1951, pp. 399, 401.)

15. See especially: G. Campori, *Pittori degli Estensi* and the other sources given in Note 3.

16. Cf. Vasari, *Milanesi*, I, p. 641 f., IV, p. 492.

17. R. Longhi, *Officina Ferrarese*, Rome, 1934, p. 12.

18. On Antonio Orsini, see L. Coletti, *Arte Veneta*, 1951, p. 94 f.

19. Cf. R. Longhi, *Officina Ferrarese*, pp. 29 f., 160. The attributions of the Smiling Madonnas were first made by the author. Versions in Ferrara (Pinacoteca and Massari collection), Cremona (Pinacoteca), New York (Metropolitan Museum), formerly Lucerne (Chillingworth collection: variant by Nicola di Maestro Antonio d'Ancona). In Cremona there is also a San Bernardino by Pelosio. Cf. E. Ruhmer, *Zeitschrift für Kunstgeschichte*, 1957, I, p. 89.

20. Panizzato and Sagramoro in 1447 (Campori, *Pittori degli Estensi*, p. 8); Pisanello in 1445 (Venturi, 'Soggiorno di Vittor Pisano alla corte estense', in *Arch. Stor. Ver.*, Dec. 1883); Galasso in 1449–50 (according to Venturi, 'L'Arte Emiliana', in *Arch. Stor. dell'Arte*, 1894, p. 89, the Galasso in question, namely Galasso di Matteo Piva, was not older than Tura). Together with Galasso, Tura made in 1451 a valuation of paintings by J. Turola (cf. Chronological List of Works, No. 1).

21. *Catalogo della Esposizione della Pittura Ferrarese*, 1933, p. 21 f.

22. On the Casa Romei see D. Zaccarini, *Casa Romei e la vita ferrarese nel secolo XV*, Ferrara, Studio ed. Ferrarese.

23. Beenken, *Rogier van der Weyden*, Munich, 1951, pp. 59, 72 f. *Idem*, 'Angelo Maccagnino' in *Preuss. Jahrbuch*', 1940, p. 150.

24. Levino, 1457; Giovanni Mille, 1472, 1474; Rubinetto, 1472, 1475, 1480; Rinaldo, 1479; see L. N. Cittadella, *Doc. ed Ill.*, 1868, pp. 166–80; Campori, *Arazzeria Estense*, 1876; A. Venturi, *Arte nel periodo di Borso*, 1885, and *Arte nel periodo d'Ercole I*, 1890. Further bibliography in Padovani, *op. cit.*, p. 623 f.

25. A. Venturi, *Storia dell'Arte*, 1914, VII, III, p. 513.

26. Longhi, *Officina*, p. 19.

27. Campori, *Pittori degli Estensi*, Modena, 1886, p. 513.

28. M. Davies, *The Earlier Italian Schools*, in National Gallery Catalogue, London, 1951, p. 188. Signed: OPVS IOHANIS ORIOLI. Giovanni was paid for a portrait of Lionello on 21 June 1447. Whether the artist is identical with Giovanni da Riolo, painter of a polyptych dated 1433 in the church of San Domenico at Imola, is doubtful (G. Ballardi, *Giovanni da Oriolo*, Florence, 1911; C. Grigioni, 'Nuovi documenti intorno a G. d. O.', in *Arte e Storia*, 1921, p. 82; *Catalogo Mostra di Melozzo*, Forlì, 1938, p. 64 f.).

29. Squarcione, in 1397; Pannonio, about 1395; Giovanni d'Allemagna, about 1400.

30. On Titolivio see, among others, L. N. Cittadella, *Doc. ed Ill.*, 1868, p. 26 f. Bono da Ferrara is known to have been active between 1441 and 1461. In each of these years he was working in Siena; in 1442 he was paid for a painting in the cupola of the cathedral in that city (L. N. Cittadella, *Doc. ed Ill.*, 1868, pp. 112, 364). In 1450 and 1452 (?) he was in Ferrara in the service of the Estes (Campori, *Pittori degli Estensi*, 1886, p. 20); he worked there in a 'studio', perhaps that at Belfiore. Two pictures are signed with his name: a *St. Jerome in a landscape* in London (Davies, 1951, p. 72 f.), in which he shows himself to have been a pupil of Pisanello, and a fresco of *St. Christopher carrying the Child Christ*, in the Ovetari chapel at Padua (destroyed). The genuineness of both signatures has been disputed and many attribute the St. Jerome to Pisanello (Longhi, *Officina*, pp. 20 f., 159; Bernhard Degenhart, *Pisanello*, Turin, 1945, p. 73). On the basis of an illuminating comparison Knapp (*Mantegna*, 1910, p. 179) added to Bono's œuvre the colossal head (reproduced as Plate 155, left) on the triumphal arch in the Ovetari chapel. The resemblance between

this head and the heads of prophets by Uccello (1443) on the clock of Florence Cathedral, would in any case point to an artist acquainted with Tuscan art, which Bono was. Another happy addition was the attribution to Bono by Longhi of a half-length Madonna in Budapest (No. 87) (*Officina*, pp. 28, 160, note 37). This would give the following development: school of Pisanello, collaboration with followers of Squarcione, influence of Piero della Francesca. Perhaps we could insert here—between the Ovetari frescoes and the Budapest *Madonna*—the much-discussed triptych from Poggibonsi near Siena (New York, Duveen Brothers), supposedly by Castagno, but in my opinion painted by Bono around 1460. In it Sienese elements (Domenico di Bartolo, Vecchietta) are combined with Paduan. This was precisely Bono's situation. Moreover, the *St. Michael* allows of much easier comparison with Bono's Ovetari frescoes than does a comparison between any part of the triptych with known works of Castagno's, and the same applies to a comparison between the head of the Madonna and the *Madonna* in Budapest (on the Poggibonsi altar-piece see G. M. Richter, 'The Beginnings of Andrea del Castagno,' in *Art in America*, October 1941, p. 177, and *Andrea del Castagno*, Chicago, 1943, p. 11 f. The complete bibliography of the triptych to date has been collected in a manuscript volume by the owner, who kindly allowed me to see it in November 1955). Very close to the Poggibonsi altar-piece are two panels formerly in the collection of Henry Harris (*John the Baptist* and a *Bishop Saint*), which also agree with the works by Bono mentioned above. Cf. E. Ruhmer, *Zeitschrift für Kunstgeschichte*, 1957, I, p. 89 f.

31. The documents relating to Pannonio can be found in L. N. Cittadella, *Documenti ed Illustrazioni*, p. 130, and in G. Campori, *Pittori degli Estensi*, p. 18; see also Venturi, *Il Periodo di Borso*, pp. 706, 708; G. Gombosi, *M. Pannonio*, Budapest Museum Annual, I, 1931; and C. Padovani, *Critica d'Arte e Pittura Ferrarese*, Rovigo, 1954, p. 543 f.

According to these documents, this painter, whose name reveals his Hungarian origin, was working for the Ferrarese court from 1415 on, producing, among other things, religious paintings and portraits of princes. By 1461 he was dead. The only certain work by him is the *Ceres* in the Museum at Budapest, signed: EX MICHAELE PANONIO, with the motto: PLANTANDI LEGES PER ME NOVERE COLONI in Latin and Greek. It is painted on wood and measures 53¾ by 32¼ inches; catalogue No. 101 (44). The *Ceres* was probably painted before Tura's *Venus*, but both belong to the same allegorical cycle. Both are generally assumed to have been

in the Studio at Belfiore, which was destroyed by fire in 1483, but it is doubtful whether they were there, since the only pictures in the Studio of which we know were the Muses executed by Angelo Maccagnino and Cosimo Tura (cf. Padovani, *op. cit.*, pp. 41, 535 f., 546). During the Baroque period, together with two other similar allegories, the *Ceres* and the *Venus*, interpreted as representing 'Summer' and 'Autumn', hung in the Palace of the Inquisition in Ferrara (Baruffaldi, *Vita di Cosimo Tura*, 1836, pp. 19, 37) and from there passed to the Costabili collection (Laderchi, *Quadreria Costabili*, 1838, p. 28, Nos. 15, 16). Both these allegories (gods, probably patrons of the months) have a parallel in graphic art: a Ferrarese engraving (Hind E III 36) from a series of representations of the months of which two have been preserved. The engraving in question shows Mars as 'March', sitting on a throne of dolphins. In composition, style and expression it is very close to the *Ceres* and the *Venus*.

The attribution to Pannonio of three panels showing saints in Milan and Ferrara (Ferrara catalogue, 1933, p. 39) seems to me doubtful (cf. Ruhmer, in *Münchener Jahrbuch*, 1954, p. 100). For the bibliography of the so-called Belfiore allegories see also M. Davies, National Gallery Catalogue, London, 1951, p. 403 f., C. Padovani, *Critica d'Arte e Pittura Ferrarese*, Rovigo, 1954, p. 535 f., and the catalogue of the Budapest museum (in Hungarian), 1954, pp. 189, 433.

32. Cf. Note 23, *Maccagnino*, 1940. According to Ciriaco's description, reproduced on p. 162, the two Ferrarese panels of *Muses* in Budapest (see Padovani, p. 43 f.), which must date from the early 1460's, cannot be identical with the much more elaborate and spiritually more ambitious Belfiore *Muses* painted by Maccagnino. On this artist see especially Cittadella, *Doc. ed Ill.*, 1868, p. 138 f. and Padovani, *op. cit.*, p. 535 f. (*ibid.*, p. 546, Ludovico Carbone's remarks on the cycle of Muses).

33. We have to distinguish between at least three artists named Galasso. The earliest, generally assumed to have been the founder of the Ferrarese school of painting, must have been born during the Trecento (he is known to have been active in 1404). An architect and sculptor named Galasso, mentioned by Superbi in *Apparato*, pp. 121, 134, worked under Leonello and Borso d'Este. The painter Galasso, who in 1451 collaborated with Tura in a valuation of works by Turola, was probably a contemporary of Tura's, active during the second half of the fifteenth century, mainly in Bologna. As no works of theirs have been preserved, it is often difficult to

distinguish between them. In the older literature the three Galassi are generally held to have been one and the same person. On the Galassi see especially Vasari, *ed. cit.*, II, 177; in the 1550 edition there is a separate 'Vita' of Galasso (I, 427f.). Cf. also Lamo, *Graticola di Bologna*, 1560 (reprinted 1844, pp. 16, 41). A complete bibliography of Galasso will be found in C. Padovani, *op. cit.*, pp. 12f., 39f., 65–9, 75–8, 95f., 172, 182, 217, 220, 229, 241, 255, 319.

Without any extant works to guide them, since Venturi several scholars have attempted to establish a hypothetical œuvre for both Galasso di Matteo Piva and Maccagnino (see notes 16, 23, 32 and also the Ferrara catalogue, 1933, p. 36). Even R. Longhi tries to do this, listing as probably by Galasso the *Woman gathering grapes* in Berlin (by Cossa) and the two *Muses* in Budapest (cf. note 32 above and also *Officina Ferrarese*, pp. 24f., 165); to Maccagnino he attributes tentatively the two *Allegories of Virtues* in the Strozzi collection, Florence (*Prudentia*, a youthful work of Cossa's, and *Spes* [?] by a pupil of Tura (Plate XIIB); in Longhi's words: 'con parti disegnate dal Tura' [*Officina*, p. 24]; both panels measure 48 × 28½ inches); a *St. Jerome doing penitence* in an unspecified private collection (*Officina*, fig. 25; *Nuovi Ampliamenti*, 1956, Plate 396), a *Madonna with angel musicians in a landscape* at Milan (*Nuovi Ampliamenti*, Florence, 1956, Plates 397–402) and the profile portrait of a lady in the Museo Civico Correr at Venice (*Nuovi Ampliamenti*, Plate 404).

34. A. Venturi, *Storia dell'Arte*, VII, III, p. 506f.

35. R. Longhi, *Vita Artistica*, 1926, p. 136.

36. E. Tietze-Conrat, *Mantegna*, London, 1955, pp. 4f., 129f. The fresco of *St. Christopher preaching* in the Ovetari chapel is signed by Ansuino. Stylistic comparisons enable us to attribute to him also the two lunette frescoes on the right wall (*St. Christopher before the King* and *St. Christopher encountering the Devil*), and one of the lunette pictures on the opposite wall (both of which are often held to be youthful works of Mantegna), representing *St. James exorcizing Demons*. Elsewhere there is the *Betrothal of St. Catherine* in the Lindenau Museum at Altenburg, which shows the influence of Filippo Lippi; and in fact, according to Vasari (life of Mantegna, Gronau ed., V, Strassburg, 1908, p. 31), Ansuino and Pizzolo worked as assistants to Filippo about 1434–7 in the Cappella del Podestà in Padua (Coletti, *Pittura Veneta*, Novara, 1953, pp. 33, 35, 81, note 49).

Nicolò Pizzolo, together with Antonio Vivarini, Giovanni d'Allemagna and Mantegna, was commissioned on 16 May 1448 to paint the Ovetari chapel. There is considerable doubt as to what was his share. It seems almost certain that he began the Assumption fresco on the east wall (cf. *Anonymus Morellianus*, ed. Frizzoni, Bologna, 1884, p. 64f.), which Mantegna altered and finished after Pizzolo's death in 1453. The three standing figures of Saints Peter, Paul and Christopher in the ceiling of the apse were likewise begun by Pizzolo and completed by Mantegna; they are often stated to be early works of Mantegna alone (Tietze-Conrat, pp. 4f., 192). If, however, as Vasari states in his life of Mantegna (ed. Gronau, V, p. 30f.), the *God the Father* and the four tondos with half-figures of Fathers of the Church beneath the buttresses of the apse are also by Pizzolo, then the stylistically similar figures of Saints Peter, Paul and Christopher must, in my opinion, also be his. Perhaps Mantegna made only a few unimportant additions. Vasari states that Pizzolo painted only a few, but also 'only good' pictures, which were considered as in no way inferior to those of Mantegna in the Ovetari chapel. If Donatello's Paduan assistant Nicolaus is identical with Nicolò Pizzolo, it might be possible to establish a small sculptural œuvre for this artist, but that is a matter which must be reserved for a later occasion.

The drawing of *Christ Blessing* in the Print Room at Berlin (No. 5060) is also attributed to Pizzolo. The *St. Jerome* in São Paulo (Fiocco, *Mantegna*, Milan, 1937) is more likely to be by Pizzolo than by Mantegna. Very close to this painting in composition and style is a drawing of *St. Jerome* in the Print Room at Berlin (No. 5114, reproduced in K. T. Parker, *North Italian Drawings*, Plate 17, p. 26). On Pizzolo see also Lazzarini, *N. Arch. Ven.*, 12, p. 161f.; V. Moschini in Thieme-Becker, Vol. 27, 1933, p. 127, and L. Coletti, *Pittura Veneta*, p. 33f.

The decorative style of Antonio Vivarini and Giovanni d'Allemagna, displayed in numerous works executed by them in collaboration, is easily recognizable in the paintings on the ceiling of the Ovetari chapel.

37. Venturi, *Storia dell'Arte*, VII, III, pp. 78, 509f.

38. B. Degenhart, 'Nach der Belliniausstellung', *Zeitschrift für Kunst*, 1950, I, p. 26f.—3⅝ × 3⅛ inches.

39. On Rizzo see, among others, Planiscig, 'Venezianische Bildhauer', *Wiener Jahrbuch*, new series I, 1926; G. Mariacher, 'Profilo di Antonio Rizzo', *Arte Veneta*, 1948, p. 67f.

40. On Ferrarese Quattrocento sculpture see especially L. N. Cittadella, *Notizie relative a Ferrara*, complete

edition 1868; and A. Venturi, *Storia dell'Arte*, VI, 'Scultura del Quattrocento'.

41. On Nicolò dell'Arca see C. Gnudi, *N. d. A.*, Turin, 1942. The relationship between Nicolò's terracotta group in Santa Maria della Vita and Tura's *Lamentation* in the Louvre has frequently attracted notice. The group may be compared with Tura's works, Plates II c, III c, 17, 57.

42. See references in Note 3. Further: Venturi, *Arte nel periodo di Borso* in *Riv. Stor. Ital.*, 1885, II, IV, and *Arte nel periodo d'Ercole I*, Bologna, 1890.
According to the sources Tura's actual circle was composed of artists of whom we know nothing but their names: the painters Filippo Ambrosi (1452), Giovanni (Bianchini?), who shared lodgings with him in 1458, Guglielmo d'Antonio, nicknamed 'il Compare', who in 1469 and 1473 procured painter's requisites for him, Teofilo di Cesena, who lived with Tura in 1486, a painter named Pellejo, whom he appointed executor of his second will, Giacomo Filippo Tealdi, or Tebaldi, who lived in Bologna; the Ferrarese painter Giovanni Matteo di Miniato Borgati (these last three in 1487); Francesco Fantinanti and Lodovico Piccolpassi (both in 1490). It should, however, also be mentioned that Tura was not the only prominent painter in Ferrara. Between 1455 and 1479 the painter Gherardo, son of Andrea da Vicenza, received far more commissions from the court than did Tura. No works by Gherardo have been preserved. See L. N. Cittadella, *Ric. e Doc.*, 1866, p. 10 f.; *id.*, *Doc. e Ill.*, 1868, pp. 108, 112, 117, 120, 132, 134, 140; Campori, *Pittori degli Estensi*, p. 13 f.; Venturi, *Periodo d'Ercole I*, p. 73 f. On Gherardo, Venturi, *Periodo di Borso*, p. 279, and *Periodo d'Ercole I*, p. 74; Campori, *Pittori degli Estensi*, p. 35.

43. Pietro Lamo, *Graticola di Bologna* (1560), reprinted Bologna, 1844, p. 31.

44. On Bellini's portrait of Leonello, see Longhi, *Officina*, 1934, p. 19. Beenken (*Rogier*, Munich, 1951, p. 72) thinks that the Este portrait in New York was a likeness of Francesco d'Este, executed about 1460 by a pupil after a drawing by Rogier.

45. Campori, *Pittori degli Estensi*, p. 13. The lost portrait by Mantegna was painted in 1449. On the back was a likeness of the court favourite Folco di Villafora.

46. Longhi, *Officina*, pp. 74, 171: about 1460-5.

47. Venturi, *Storia dell'Arte*, VII, III, p. 546: about the middle of the 1470's; according to Longhi, *Officina*, p. 161, a workshop production.

48. Longhi, *Ampliamenti nell'Officina Ferrarese*, Florence, 1940, p. 5: about 1470.

49. K. T. Parker, *North Italian Drawings*, London, 1927, pp. 13, 28.

50. *Rogier van der Weyden*, Munich, 1951, p. 72.

51. S. Ortolani, *Tura, Cossa, Roberti*, Milan, 1941, p. 28: 'soon after 1450'.

52. Ortolani (*op. cit.*, p. 25) speaks of 'modern embellishments', probably referring to the head. Longhi, however (*Officina*, p. 26), sees in the head reminiscences of Rogier, which would make it the older, not the newer portion. M. Davies thinks that it was painted by a follower of Tura influenced by Rogier (National Gallery Catalogue, London, 1951, p. 404). Ortolani believes that the picture has some connection with the commission Tura received between 1477 and 1481. (Cf. Chronological List of Works, No. 52.)

53. Thus interpreted by H. Beenken (*Preussisches Jahrbuch*, 1940, p. 152 f.). The format of both the panels in Florence is 48 × 28½ inches (it is quite likely that all the so-called Belfiore *Allegories* were cut down). A. Venturi, in 1890, attributed the Florentine panels to Pannonio (*Periodo d'Ercole*, p. 35, note 3); Gombosi (*Burlington Magazine*, February 1933, p. 66 f.) and Beenken (*loc. cit.*) assigned them hypothetically to Angelo Maccagnino.

54. The attribution is mine. A. Venturi, *Storia dell'-Arte*, VII, III, p. 570, assigns it to a follower of Tura; Longhi, *Officina*, p. 24, to Maccagnino (?). That it is really an early work by Cossa dating from the early 1460's becomes clear if we compare it with the *Madonna*, certainly painted by Cossa, in the National Gallery, Washington. Tura's influence can be seen in the richness and mobility of the sweep of the folds.

55. See Chronological List of Works, No. 52.

56. Inventory No. 2579. Pen drawing, 12¾ × 9¾ inches. Cf. Catalogue 1941, VI, No. 3. According to Wickhoff, school of Cossa. An engraving of St. Justina attributed to Nicoletto da Modena (Hind, Nicoletto, No. 4, Cat. II, p. 114) is very close to this drawing; it too shows traces of Tura's influence.

57. *Officina*, pp. 35 f., 160. Ortolani agrees (*Tura, Cossa, Roberti*, p. 77 f.), but points out that in the principal panel in Ajaccio the 'Belfiore atmosphere' is predominant.

58. Longhi, *Officina*, p. 40. Venturi (*L'Arte*, 1930, p. 238), attributes it to Tura, as does Ortolani (*op. cit.*, p. 64). The portrait should be compared with the half-length of *St. Cosmas* in the Rijksmuseum, Amsterdam, by Bartolomeo Vivarini. It is impossible to make a definite attribution, but of the various possibilities, the name of Tura is the most likely.

59. Ortolani (*op. cit.*, p. 34) connects it with Tura's decorations for the library at Mirandola and dates it about 1466. From the point of view of content, the figure does not fit into the programme of the cycle. In composition and conception of the body-forms the 'Caritas' resembles a drawing of a likewise winged figure of 'Fortuna' in the Kunsthalle at Hamburg (Inventory No. 21 507r), which must be attributed to Marco Zoppo (pen and wash, $9\frac{7}{8} \times 8\frac{1}{8}$ inches). Although Zoppo was certainly not an imitator of Tura, nevertheless he often copied the works of other artists, e.g. Mantegna, so that in this case he may have copied Tura (cf. fig. 11).

60. See note 5 above and Hermann, *Jahrbuch d. AH. Kaiserhauses*, 1898, XIX, p. 207 f.); see also Venturi, *Preussisches Jahrbuch*, 1888, p. 10 ff.

61. Contrary to Hermann, A. Venturi assumes that there were ten panels, not divided (*Preussisches Jahrbuch*, 1888, p. 10 f.). In an appendix to Venturi's article (p. 38), Harck wrongly describes the Mirandola pictures as frescoes. On the decoration of the library see also Campori, *Artisti . . . negli Stati Estensi*, Modena, 1854, p. 473.

62. Serafino, in MarcAntonio Guarini, *Compendio Istorico*, 1621, p. 90; see also R. Longhi, *Officina*, p. 7; Alberti, *Officina*, p. 12. It was not until 1932 that Alberti's frescoes were transferred from the church to the Pinacoteca (Padovani, *Critica d'Arte e Pittura Ferrarese*, Rovigo, 1954, p. 13).

63. L. N. Cittadella, *Ricordi e Documenti . . .*, Ferrara, 1866, p. 26 f.

64. On Costa's frescoes see Vasari, *Vite*, 1550, I, p. 428; G. Baruffaldi, *Vite*, I, pp. 109, 220; C. Cittadella, *Catalogo Istorico*, 1782, I, p. 85; and C. Laderchi, *Pittura*

Ferrarese, 1857, p. 42. Rather curiously, the descriptions correspond exactly with those of Tura's Sacrati chapel, so that the information must be considered unreliable (see notes to No. 27 of the list of works). According to Superbi (*Apparato de gli Hvomini Illustri*, Ferrari, 1620, p. 122) the choir of San Domenico contained seventeenth-century frescoes by Bastianino. On the sculptures in San Domenico see Baruffaldi, *Vite*, I, p. 220 ('Alfonso Lombardi'). On the intarsia-work see A. Venturi, *I primordi del Rinascimento artistico a Ferrara*, Turin, 1884, p. 30.

65. Scarsellino's picture is in the fifth chapel on the left; it is a large canvas of elongated format.

66. Venturi dates these tondi about 1470 (*Storia*, VII, III, p. 530 f.), Ortolani, after 1480 (*op. cit.*, p. 71 f.), while B. Nicolson (*The Painters of Ferrara*, London, 1950, p. 11) assigns them to the second half of the 1470's.

67. Longhi, *Officina*, pp. 34, 160, and Ortolani, *Tura, Cossa, Roberti*, p. 20 f.

68. With the aid of a number of older copies, and especially of the excellent inventory copies by Giuseppe Mazzolani (1903–9), drawings from which by Edmondo Fontana are preserved in the Museo Schifanoia. A useful aid is also the general scheme, which can be deduced with reasonable accuracy from the parts preserved. It would seem that the frescoes on the south and west walls needed restoration as soon as they had been finished, which was probably due in part to the employment of unsuccessful experimental methods. In the eighteenth century all the walls were whitewashed; they were partially freed from the whitewash at the beginning of the nineteenth century and completely freed, by A. Compagnoni, in 1840 (C. Laderchi, *Pittura Ferrarese*, 1857, p. 31).

69. Practically all the stylistic analyses hitherto made distinguish five separate hands, but in each case the groups are variously distributed and assigned to other artists. Summaries of all the important earlier descriptions in G. Bargellesi, *Palazzo Schifanoia*, Bergamo, 1945, p. 12 f., and C. Padovani, *Critica d'Arte e Pittura Ferrarese*, Rovigo, 1954, pp. 202 f., 483–533.

70. Cossa from his own letters, dated 25 March 1470 (published in *Der Kunstfreund*, 9, 1, V, by Venturi); Baldassare, from a list of works in the Archivio di Stato, Modena (*Erculis I epistolarum registrum*, 1473; cf. Venturi,

Periodo d'Ercole, 1890, p. 58). Further bibliography in Padovani, *op. cit.*, pp. 206, 305, 495 f.

71. By him, in the Palazzo Schifanoia, are the representations of the months of June, July and August, with the exception of certain parts of the last two, the pictures between July and August, the fresco to the left of September, and the ceiling. Longhi (*Officina*, pp. 58, 168) also mentions Cicognara's name, but curiously enough he attributes to him in the Hall of the Months only the representation of August. Moreover he thinks that we must distinguish between two artists named Cicognara (p. 165 f.). In a manner which is not very clear he also derives from the August master a 'Maestro dagli occhi spalancati' (so designated by Venturi) and a 'Maestro dagli occhi ammiccanti', adding to the œuvre of the latter one of the 'Smiling Madonnas' (Ferrara, Pinacoteca), though this is certainly by Francesco Pelosio. To judge by his other works, Pelosio can hardly be considered as one of the Schifanoia painters. Except for the *Madonna*, all these works are in my opinion by the hand of one and the same master: Antonio Cicognara. (See E. Ruhmer, *Zeitschrift für Kunstgeschichte*, 1957, I, p. 94 f.)

72. This attribution finds support in Longhi, who identifies his 'Vicino da Ferrara' as Baldassare d'Este (*Officina*, 1934, pp. 28, 78 f., 165 f.; *Ampliamenti*, 1940, p. 13 f.; *Nuovi Ampliamenti*, 1956, p. 166 f.). The *St. George* by 'Vicino', reproduced as Fig. 28 in his *Ampliamenti*, agrees in every respect with the knights in the Schifanoia fresco (cf. E. Ruhmer, *Zeitschrift für Kunstgeschichte*, 1957, I, p. 95 f.).
Of the numerous portraits and altar-pieces by Baldassare mentioned in the sources, only a few have been preserved: a portrait of Borso in the Castello at Milan (546); one of Tito Strozzi in a private collection at Venice; the above-mentioned portions of the Schifanoia fresco and three portrait medals of Ercole I made in 1472. On the basis of what we already know, it is possible to attribute to Baldassare, in addition to the 'Vicino' *St. George*, two portraits, one of them in the Musée Jacquemart-André, Paris, and one at Châalis; the portrait of Cosimo Pasetti in the Museo Stibbert, Florence, and a *Christ bearing the Cross* (half-length) in the Bonomi collection, Milan (Photo Fiorentini 3065). According to eighteenth-century chroniclers, there were other works, allegedly signed by Baldassare, in the sacristy of Ferrara cathedral, in Santa Maria degli Angeli, Sant'Antonio in Polesine, Santa Caterina, Santa Maria della Consolazione and in private collections. Doubtful is the attribution to 'Vicino alias Baldassare'

of a group of pictures connected with a large *Crucifixion* in the Musée des Arts décoratifs in Paris (others in the Strozzi collection and the Museo Bardini at Florence, at Bergamo and elsewhere); in many respects these remind one of the early Bianchi Ferrari.

73. *Vita di Cosimo Tura*, printed at Ferrara in 1836; chapter on Tura in *Vite de' Pittori etc.*, printed in 1844.

74. This is the opinion of Cavalcaselle, Harck, Gruyer and others. Cf. note 69 above.

75. *Periodo di Borso*, p. 689 f.; *idem*, 'Gli affreschi del Palazzo Schifanoia' in *Atti e Mem. . . . Romagna*, II, 1885, p. 3.

76. In *Jahrbuch der Preuss. Kunstsammlungen*, 1888, p. 4 f.

77. If this fresco were by Ercole, his subsequent development would be retrogressive, which is hardly credible. The altar-piece from Ravenna (1480–1) in the Brera, which is certainly by Roberti, for all its beauty is far more hesitant in invention and execution than the 'September' painted in 1469–70.

78. The interpretation of the Schifanoia frescoes is based mainly on the following works: A. Warburg, 'Italienische Kunst und internationale Astrologie', in Vol. II of his *Gesammelte Schriften* (1932); W. Gundel, *Dekane and Dekanbilder*, Glückstadt-Hamburg, 1936; J. Carson Webster, *The Labours of the Months*, Princeton, 1938.

79. Ed. Salani, Florence, 1932, VII, pp. 322 f., 325, 345, etc.

80. To judge from his clothing, the man to whom Borso is speaking in the loggia, is a Venetian (Gruyer, 'Le palais de Schifanoia' in *Revue des deux mondes*, August 1883, p. 618: Paolo Morosini).
On the disturbed relations between Ferrara and Venice about 1470, see especially G. B. Pigna, *Historia de' Principi di Este*, Venice, 1572, pp. 742 f., 744, 735 f.

81. This is probably the origin of the usual designation 'Lussuria', in contradiction with Manilius, whom we otherwise follow here and who assigns Vulcan to September.

82. 'Domenico filio Jacobi Valerj libras quinquaginta, et omnia designa, et alia que spectant ad artem pictoriam' (L. N. Cittadella, *Ric. e documenti intorno alla vita di C. Tura*, Ferrara, 1866).

83. The Vienna drawing: Inventory No. 33, pen and wash, 10⅞ × 8⅜ inches; the drawing in the Ambrosiana: pen on pink paper, 5¾ × 5 inches. The former is variously attributed to Lazzaro Vasari, copy after Castagno, Pollaiuolo, copy after Pollaiuolo (cf. Wickhoff, *Albertina*, 1932, III, p. 5; Berenson, *Drawings of the Florentine Painters*, Chicago, 1938, II, p. 267, No. 1909); the Milan drawing is attributed to the school of Pisanello. A facsimile edition of the Zoppo sketchbook was published by Campbell Dodgson, London, 1923; for further references see Popham and Pouncey, *Italian Drawings in the British Museum: The fourteenth and fifteenth Centuries*, London, 1950, p. 162.

84. See Note 38, above. In addition to his works in Palazzo Schifanoia and at Belriguardo, Tura is said to have painted a fresco (a lunette containing a *Madonna*) for Santa Maria degli Angeli (C. Cittadella, *Cat. Ist.*, I, 1782, p. 54), but this statement by a chronicler cannot be considered reliable.

85. Hill 102 (*A Corpus of Italian Medals before Cellini*, London, 1930).

86. The bust in Ferrara (Palazzo Marfisa d'Este) dates from 1475; the relief in the Louvre shows Ercole at the same age and bears the inscription OPVS SPERANDEI. In their lives of Lorenzo Costa both Vasari and Baruffaldi (*Vite*, I, p. 108) mention the collection of portraits of the Estensian princes: the Este portraits there attributed to Costa were certainly painted by Tura, Baldassare d'Este, Cossa, Roberti and other artists.

87. Wart Arslan, in *Zeitschrift für Kunstgeschichte*, V, 1934, p. 174; *idem, Inventario degli oggetti d'Arte*, VII, Provincia di Padova, 1936, p. 24. Height 22¾ inches.

88. See Chronological List of Works, No. *64*.

89. Cologne: 97·5 × 207 cm.; Cleveland: 112 × 216 cm. Lit.: Dorothy G. Shepherd in *Cleveland Bulletin*, 38, 1951, p. 40f.; Ortolani (*op. cit.*, p. 76) thinks that the figures are portraits of Acarino, Ercole I, Isabella and Beatrice d'Este or Anna Sforza, and relates the tapestry to the terracotta Sepolcro of Guido Mazzoni, dating from 1485, in Santa Maria della Rosa, Ferrara.

90. The Ferrara Exhibition Catalogue, 1933, p. 205, speaks of a relationship to Tura. Van Marle (*Apollo*, XXI, 1935, p. 12) suggests, without giving reasons,

Domenico di Paris. The *Pietà* was formerly in the Ventura collection in Florence, but was sold in 1940.

91. See note 38 above. Four paintings by Tura representing Fathers (or Doctors) of the Church are said to have been at one time in the Zafferini collection, Ferrara.

92. Popham-Pouncey, *Italian Drawings in the British Museum*, London, 1950, No. 256, catalogue p. 158.

93. According to Longhi, by Tura (*Officina*, p. 39); Ortolani (p. 69) dates it about 1475.

94. T. Borenius in *Burlington Magazine*, XXVII, p. 202.

95. There is an old repetition or copy in the Art Institute, Chicago. The drawing in the Drey collection (catalogue No. 406), certainly authentic as regards its construction, may have been a preliminary sketch for further repaintings. Ortolani (p. 40) dates the picture about 1468. (See Plates VIII and IX.)

96. See note 14 above and Notes on Plates 50–9.

97. *Vite*, I, p. 77f.

98. Superbi, *Apparato degli Hvomini Illustri*, Ferrara, 1620, p. 122.

99. M. Davies, National Gallery Catalogue, *Earlier Italian Schools*, London, 1951, p. 400, and R. Longhi, *Officina*, p. 36.

100. The inscription was only partially legible as early as 1706, but Baruffaldi gives the whole text (*Vite*, I, p. 78).

101. Venturi (*Storia*, VII, III, p. 532f.). On the other hand Longhi (*Officina*, p. 39) maintains that it is unlikely that the same saint, Maurelius, would have appeared twice in one and the same altar-piece. Ortolani (p. 70f.) assigns them to Duke Ercole I's little private altar, executed in 1475.

102. *Officina*, Plate 45. Longhi describes as parts of the predella the three tondi with scenes from the childhood of Christ in Cambridge, Boston and New York. B. Nicolson (*The Painters of Ferrara*, London, 1950, p. 11) disagrees and dates the tondi later, about 1476–80.

103. On Bernardino da Venezia and Amadio da Milano, see L. N. Cittadella, *Documenti ed illustrazioni*, Ferrara, 1868, pp. 125 and 161.

104. These bronzes and the stylistically similar *Virgin* seem to be by Giovanni Baroncelli, the *St. John* and the *St. George* by Domenico di Paris, but the *Crucified Christ* was probably made by Nicolò Baroncelli, who died in 1453.

105. C. Padovani, *Critica d'Arte e Pitt. Ferr.*, Rovigo, 1954, S.535f.

106. Baruffaldi, *Vita di Cosimo Tura*, p. 37, note; C. Laderchi, *Quadreria Costabili*, I, 1838, p. 27, No. 13. Ortolani (*op. cit.*, p. 61) doubts whether the two panels have any connection and thinks that the *Christ on the Cross* is a fragment of a lost *St. Francis receiving the Stigmata*. That such a painting by Tura existed, is not to be excluded. C. Cittadella (*Cat. Ill.*, II, p. 211f.) describes a painting of St. Francis, allegedly by Tura, which about 1780 was in the Rizzoni collection at Ferrara, in the following words: 'Un S. Francesco, grande al naturale, che nel monte d'Alvernia riceve le sagre stimmate, dipinto con somma esattezza.' It is possible that the main features of this painting have been preserved in the Tura-like miniature of the *Stigmatization of St. Francis* from the Wildenstein collection, Paris, in which the Christ is similar to the Brera fragment, though with cherub's wings. Nevertheless, the previous existence of a *St. Francis* by Tura is not a valid reason for separating the Brera fragment from the painting in London, since the crucifix is also an attribute of St. Jerome and from the artistic point of view both portions agree. Lastly, G. Bargellesi has produced concrete arguments to prove that the Milan fragment belongs to the London picture (*Notizie di opere d'arte ferrarese*, Rovigo, 1955, p. 17f.).

107. L. N. Cittadella, *Notizie relative a Ferrara*, 1868, I, pp. 569, 706.

108. C. Ricci (*Rassegna d'Arte*, V, 1905, p. 145f.) connects the *Sebastian* in Berlin, the *Anthony* in Paris, the *Madonna* in Bergamo (centre portion), the *Dominic* in Florence and the *Christopher* in Berlin with the altarpiece of San Luca in Borgo, without considering the differences in proportions and composition or the circumstance that we have no proof that a *Madonna* was executed for San Luca.

109. There is a description of the San Romano altarpiece, together with that of San Luca in Borgo, in Baruffaldi (*Vite*, I, p. 76f.). The San Romano altar-piece is also mentioned by C. Barotti (*Pitture e Sculture*, Ferrara, 1770, p. 95), and C. Cittadella (*Cat. Ist.*, I, 1782,

p. 54). From these sources we learn that both these altar-pieces consisted of 'many parts with separate pictures of all sorts of single figures of saints on a gold ground'. The altar-piece from San Giacomo in Terra d'Argenta attributed to Tura must have been very similar, for C. Cittadella (*Cat. Ist.*, I, p. 55) describes it as 'a painting with ornaments, and saints standing around the image of Maria Santissima'. Although the Madonna is here expressly stated to have been a separate picture, Ricci (cf. note 108) assumes that the composition was a kind of Sacra Conversazione on one panel. B. Nicolson, *The Painters of Ferrara*, London, 1950, p. 11, believes on the other hand that all the paintings shown in Plates 72–82 belonged to the San Giacomo altar-piece. The problematic nature of all these statements and the consequences to be deduced from them becomes clear when we learn that G. Scalabrini (in Baruffaldi, *Vite*, I, p. 76, note by Petrucci) knew of a triptych by Tura from San Romano, consisting of St. Jerome, St. Sebastian and St. John. Two of the panels are said to have passed to the Barbicinti collection, Ferrara (No. 180) and one of these, the St. Jerome (on wood, $39\frac{3}{8} \times 6\frac{7}{8}$ inches), is now in the Pinacoteca at Ferrara. But it is not by Tura (see Padovani, *Critica etc.*, 1954, p. 156).

The altar-piece from San Guglielmo, Ferrara, likewise attributed to Tura, must have been of a different kind. Barotti's description (*Pitture e Sculture*, 1770, p. 108) leads one to suppose that it comprised as many as seven main panels, on which saints were shown in half-length; in the middle was St. William, with Saints Lucia, Apollonia and Agatha on one side of him and 'altri Santi' on the other; in addition there were predella panels (of which Barotti mentions six) showing scenes from the lives of saints and a Last Supper. A high altar was consecrated in San Guglielmo in 1489 (cf. Guarini, *Comp. Ist.*, 1621, p. 218).

According to Barotti (*op. cit.*, p. 125) and Scalabrini (*Chiese di Ferrara*, 1773, p. 181f.), single panels of saints —parts of another polyptych (?)—were to be seen on the side walls of the Trotti chapel in San Francesco, Ferrara; they represented Saints Florentinus, Antoninus and Bernardino.

Although these attributions are by no means binding, there is no particular reason why they should be rejected. If out of so large a number of altar-pieces only a few panels by Tura have survived the last 150 years, that could be partially explained by the fact that the altar-pieces were not executed in their entirety by Tura. Just as the alleged Tura triptych from San Vito was completed by Lorenzo Costa, so can we also assume that Tura occasionally provided additions for older altar-pieces or others painted by another hand.

110. See note 113.

111. Baruffaldi (*Vite*, I, p. 76) gives 1434 as the date of execution and maintains that he found this date in the church archives. If this is the date of a work by Tura, then there must have been a misreading or a slip of the pen, and in fact it is easy to confuse a 3 with an 8. The date 1484 is also acceptable for pictures which are very similar to the *St. Anthony* in Modena.
Although O. Härtzsch (*Tura*, pp. 3, 5, 11, 19, 21, 29) dates all these panels about 1470 or about 1475, and only the Nantes panel in the 1480's, Nicolson (*The Painters of Ferrara*, p. 11f.) thinks that it would be more correct to date all of them about 1482.

112. On some variants of the *Pietà* composition see the Notes on Plates 78–82.

113. Letter dated 8 January 1490, in which Tura complains that he has not yet been paid for the picture delivered 'da sey anni' (Venturi, *Storia*, VII, III, p. 519f.)

114. *Catalogo Istorico*, I, p. 51; see also R. Pallucchini, *Catalogue*, 1952, p. 84.

115. Catalogue of the Ferrara Exhibition, 1933, p. 68 (reproduced).

116. National Gallery, No. 905, on wood, $17\frac{3}{4} \times 13\frac{3}{8}$ inches. Generally considered to be by Tura's own hand.—In his *Nuovi Ampliamenti* (Plate 406) Longhi reproduces a fragment showing two angel musicians in the Colonna collection in Rome, describing it as a work by Tura finished by another hand or repainted; it is difficult to discover any traces of Tura in this painting.

117. Museo Poldi Pezzoli, No. 627, on wood, $8\frac{5}{8} \times 9\frac{7}{8}$ inches. According to the catalogue, Crowe-Cavalcaselle, Bertini and Morassi attribute it to Tura. The weak execution of the part of the headdress hanging down over the shoulder makes this attribution doubtful. Another alleged Tura, a male portrait, is reproduced by Longhi in his *Nuovi Ampliamenti* (Plate 405; Châalis, Musée Jacquemart-André), but this is certainly by Baldassare d'Este (cf. note 72).

118. A drawing from the Oppenheimer Collection, now in the British Museum, 'The Infant Christ blessing', pen and brown ink with washes in yellow, green, and red ($3\frac{5}{8} \times 3\frac{1}{4}$ inches) has been discussed as by Tura or from his workshop (K. T. Parker, *North Italian Drawings*, 1927, p. 27; O. Härtzsch, *Tura*, 1931, p. 43); but the Catalogue of the British Museum (*Italian Drawings: The fourteenth and fifteenth Centuries*, by Popham and Pouncey, London, 1950, p. 206) states rightly: 'The drawing seems to be a deliberate *pastiche*, of such low quality and such apparently late date that it may be called a forgery.'

119. Catalogue of the New York Exhibition, 1924. On wood, $16\frac{1}{2} \times 11\frac{3}{4}$ inches.

120. See note 95 above.

121. See notes 3 and 82 above.

122. On Ferrarese miniature-painting see C. Laderchi, *Pittura Ferrarese*, 1857, p. 31f.; L. N. Cittadella, *Doc. ed Ill.*, 1866, pp. 146, 172, 175f., 179f.; idem, *Ric. e Doc.*, 1868, p. 12; J. Hermann, in *Jahrbuch d. AH. Kaiserhauses*, XXI, pp. 72f., 209f.; Hermanin, in *L'Arte*, III, p. 356f.; Venturi, *Arte nel Periodo di Borso*, 1885, p. 730f.; von Harck, in *Arch. Stor.*, I, p. 104f.; d'Ancona, in *L'Arte*, XIII, p. 5f.; Wescher, in *Berliner Museen, Amtl. Berichte*, 51, p. 78f.; Ortolani, *Tura, Cossa, Roberti*, Milan, 1941, p. 25f.; P. della Pergola, *Franco de' Russi*, in Thieme-Becker, *Künstlerlexikon*; L. Baer, *Guglielmo Giraldi*, ibid. Detailed bibliography in Padovani, *op. cit.*, pp. 18f., 44, 321, 573, 580, 583, 586f., 596–600, 610. The miniature by Franco de' Russi (?) reproduced is: Rome, Biblioteca Vaticana, Cod. Urb. lat. 151, fol. 6 (portrait of Pope Paul II); the miniature by Jacopo Filippo d'Argenta (?) is in a codex now in the Museo del Duomo, Ferrara.

123. Reproduced in H. Salmi, *Bollettino d'Arte*, 1926, p. 218.

124. R. Longhi, *Ampliamenti*, Florence, 1940, Plate 28. Said to have come from the Costabili collection (as a 'Tura'). In 1782 C. Cittadella (*Catalogo Istorico*, IV, p. 308) owned a 'tavola per longo con un S. Giorgio', allegedly by Tura. Cf. notes 70 and 72, above.

125. Cf. note 54, above.

126. The painter of the *Madonna between St. John the Evangelist and the Beato Bertoni* (probably 1484) in the Pinacoteca at Faenza and of a number of other works at Faenza, Paris (Louvre) and Edinburgh (National Gallery). On Scaletti, see the *Catalogue* of the Melozzo exhibition, Forlì, 1938, p. 85f.

127. On wood, $67\frac{1}{4} \times 33\frac{1}{2}$ inches. Gemäldegalerie, No. 42A. Formerly attributed to Cossa, but assigned by Laderchi to Costa as early as 1838 (*Quadreria Costabili*,

I, p. 39). Under Tura's name in Berenson, *Pitture Italiane del Rinascimento*, Milan edition, 1936.

128. C. Cittadella, *Catalogo Istorico*, II, p. 212.

129. On wood, 26½ × 14½ inches. On the back is the old, but not authentic inscription: 'Opera di Cosmo Turi altri... detto Gosmè pittor celebre Ferrar...' etc. From the Crispi collection, Ferrara (1667–1745), where it was described as a 'Cossa' (see Scalabrini, *Inventario delle pitture di Mons. G. Crispi*). Attributed to Tura by Lionello Venturi in the catalogue of the Gualino collection, Turin-Rome 1926, No. 23. According to B. Nicolson, *The Painters of Ferrara*, London, 1950, pp. 14, 20, it is by Ercole Roberti. Until 1939 in the Italian Embassy in London (M. de Benedetti, 'Notes on Italian paintings at the Italian Embassy', in *Apollo*, XX, 1934, p. 303); now in the Galleria Sabauda, Turin.

130. On wood, 14 × 22¾ × 10½ inches. Reggio Emilia, Museo Civico. According to Venturi, (*Storia*, VII, III, p. 1048f.) it was painted by the Degli Erri brothers of Modena; Longhi (*Officina*, p. 161) attributes it to Martino da Modena (a miniaturist).

The artist's signature, in a letter of 1490

Plate I. Virgin and Sleeping Child (see Plate 8). *Venice, Academy.*

a

b

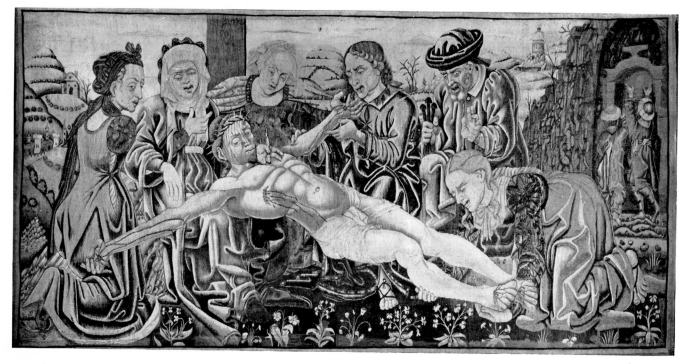

c

Plate II. (a) Angels holding the symbol of St. Bernardinus. Lunette of the 'Virgin with Sleeping Child' (see Plate I). *Venice, Academy*. (b) Follower of Tura: Painted wooden chest. *Reggio Emilia, Museo Civico*. (c) The Lamentation over Christ. Tapestry from a design by Tura. *Cleveland (Ohio), Museum of Art*.

a

b

c

Plate III. (a) Tura: Detail from the fresco of 'September'. *Ferrara, Palazzo Schifanoia.* (b) Ercole Roberti: 'The Massacre of the Innocents'. Detail from the Ravenna altar-piece. *Milan, Brera.* (c) The Lamentation over Christ. Tapestry from a design by Tura. *Cologne, Neven-Dumont Collection.*

Plate IV. Studio of Tura: Fragment of an Annunciation. *London, National Gallery.*

Plate V. Unknown Master: Charity. (The three children painted by Tura.) *Milan, Museo Poldi Pezzoli.*

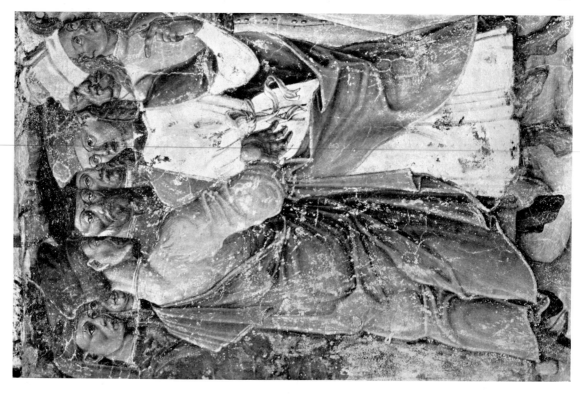

b

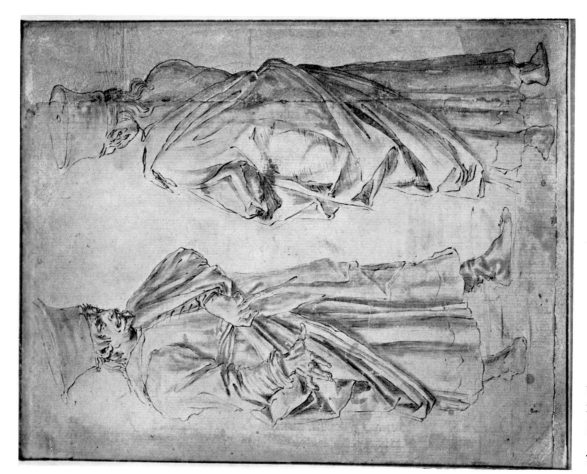

a

Plate VI. (a) Close to Tura: Two Orientals. Drawing. *Vienna, Albertina.* (b) Antonio Cicognara: Detail from the fresco of 'June'. *Ferrara, Palazzo Schifanoia.*

Plate VII. (a) Tura: Vesta. Drawing, reworked by another hand. *Vienna, Albertina.* (b) Antonio Cicognara: Detail from the fresco of 'August'. *Ferrara, Palazzo Schifanoia.*

Plate VIII. After Tura: Pietà (see Plate 47). *Chicago, Art Institute (Ryerson Collection).*

Plate IX. Tura: Pietà (see Plate 47). Fragment of a drawing, reworked by a later hand. *London, M. H. Drey Collection.*

Plate X. (a) Niccolò Pizzolo: St. Gregory. Fresco. (Destroyed in 1944.) *Padua, Eremitani, Ovetari Chapel.* (b) Detail from a Ferrarese miniature: Pope Paul II. *Rome, Biblioteca Vaticana, Cod. Urb. lat. 151, fol. 6.* (c) Tura or Giovanni Bellini (?): A Doctor of the Church. Drawing. *Bayonne, Musée Bonnat.*

a

b

c

Plate XI. (a) Jacopo Filippo d'Argenta (?): St. Francis. Initial from a missal. *Ferrara, Museo della Cattedrale.*
(b) Imitator of Tura: Madonna and Sleeping Child. *Formerly Rome, Paolini Collection.* (c) Lorenzo Costa: St. Sebastian.
Dresden, Gallery.

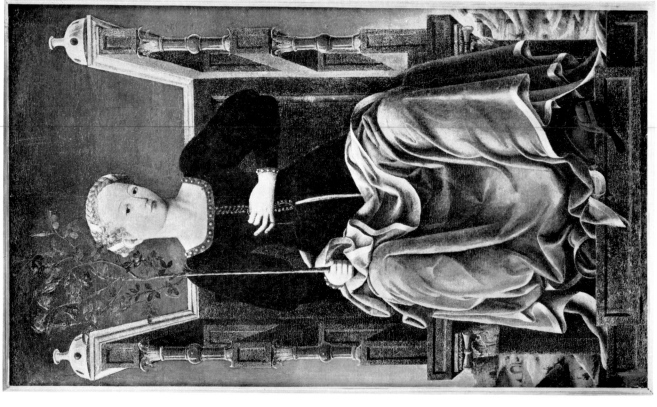

Plate XII. (a) Pupil of Tura: Virgin and Child. *Turin, Galleria Sabauda.* (b) Tura and a Pupil: Allegory of Hope ('Spes'). *Florence, Strozzi Collection.*

a

b

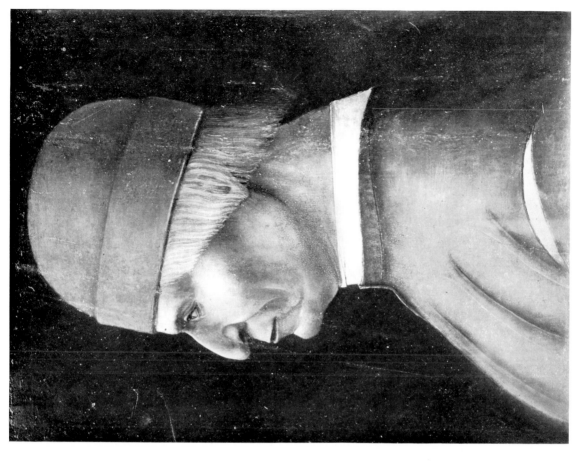

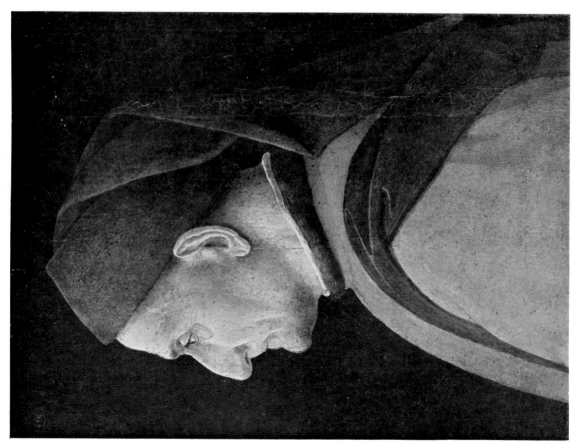

a

b

Plate XIII. (a) Studio of Tura: Portrait of an Old Man. *Milan, Museo Poldi Pezzoli.* (b) Baldassare d'Este: Portrait of an Old Man. *Châalis, Musée Jacquemart-André.*

Plate XIV. Cossa and Roberti: Altarpiece from St. Lazzaro. (Destroyed in 1945.) *Formerly Berlin, Kaiser Friedrich Museum.*

Plate XV. Ansuino da Forlì: St. Christopher preaching. Fresco. (Destroyed in 1944.) *Formerly Padua, Eremitani, Ovetari Chapel.*

Plate XVI. Michele Pannonio: Allegorical Figure (Ceres). *Budapest, Museum of Fine Arts.*

CHRONOLOGICAL LIST OF TURA'S WORKS

Unless otherwise stated, the documents relating to Tura's works, almost all of which are in the Archivio di Stato, Modena, will be found reproduced either wholly or in part in the following works:

L. N. CITTADELLA, *Notizie relative a Ferrara*, I and II, Ferrara, 1868.

L. N. CITTADELLA, *Ricordi e documenti intorno alla vita di Cosimo Tura*, Ferrara, 1866.

G. CAMPORI, *L'Arazzeria Estense*, Modena, 1876.

A. VENTURI, *L'Arte nel periodo di Borso d'Este, Rivista Storica Italiana*, 1885, II, IV, p. 689f.

G. CAMPORI, *I pittori degli Estensi*, Modena, 1886.

A. VENTURI, 'Cosma Tura genannt Cosmè', *Jahrbuch der Preussischen Kunstsammlungen*, 1888, p. 3f.

A. VENTURI, *L'Arte nel periodo d'Ercole I*, Bologna, 1890.

If the number denoting the work is in italics, this means that it has been lost. Extant works of which there is no documentary evidence in the sources are not dated in the list below and appear at that point to which it is possible to assign them in accordance with Tura's stylistic development.

1451

1. Tura begins working for the Ferrarese court. According to Campori, 1886, p. 23, he painted twenty-four small banners for the castle, but Venturi, 1888, p. 3, note 1, thinks that this refers to a valuation made by Tura and Galasso of some small banners for trumpets which Jacopo Turola had decorated with Duke Borso's coats of arms. If Tura acted as a valuer at the age of twenty-one, he must have made a name for himself as an artist before that date.

2. *Portrait of a youthful prince of the House of Este*. New York, Metropolitan Museum.   PLATE I

1452

3. Tura decorates a helmet for the winner at a tournament held on St. George's day. The decoration consisted of a unicorn, one of the Estensian emblems, dipping its horn in a stream; above it, a palm tree. Payment was made on 22 April 1452 (Venturi, 1888, p. 4, note 6).

1452

4. For the Ferrarese tailors' guild Tura paints a banner, which he had to modify in 1456. Delivery was made on 21 August 1456 (Cittadella, 1866, pp. 24, 28, 29; Campori, 1886, p. 23).

1452

5. Tura has a share in the painting and gilding of seventeen caskets, adorned with small pictures by Giorgio d'Allemagna and nutmeg reliefs by Giovanni Carlo di Bretagna, representing, among other things: 'figure del nostro Signore e nostra dona e passione', together with heraldic devices of Duke Borso (Venturi, 1885, p. 710, note 2).

1457

6. Tura receives twenty-one ells of canvas, colours and six sheets of paper, to be used for making designs and coloured cartoons for tapestries to serve as bench-coverings and door-curtains. Subject: 'arme et devixe' of Duke Borso, viz. 'paraduro, alicorno, batesmo et la chiodara', to be surrounded by decorations containing foliage and animals ('diversi animalj et verdure'). The work was executed by the weaver Levino di Francia. Payments were made to Tura on 18 May and 29 July.

1458

7. Tura receives forty-seven sheets of paper to be used for making drawings for bench-coverings. Subject: Borso's heraldic devices (Venturi, 1888, p. 8).

1458 (?)

8. Date beneath a *Nativity* in the old sacristy of Ferrara cathedral, which Tura is said to have painted by order of the bailiff Vincenzo de' Lardi. The composition consisted of numerous small figures. In the eighteenth century it was transferred to the main sacristy and must therefore have been an altar-piece. No trace of the picture remains (C. Barotti, *Pitture e sculture . . . di Ferrara,*

1770, p. 44; L. Lanzi, *Storia pittorica*, Bassano, 1795–6; Cittadella, 1866, p. 8).

1459–63

9. As 'depintore del Studio', Tura plays a leading role in the execution of numerous paintings for Borso's 'studio' in the castle of Belfiore, on the northern outskirts of Ferrara. On 31 October 1459 he receives the first supply of colours and in the Spring of 1463 the last. For the most part it was a matter of decorative paintings on walls and furniture. Tura's *Venus* in London (No. 21) is generally held to be one of the works painted for Belfiore, though it is doubtful whether this is correct. According to Lodovico Carbone, for Belfiore Tura completed the cycle of nine *Muses* which Angelo Maccagnino began by painting two panels (*De amoenitate, utilitate, magnificentia Herculei Barchi*; cf. L. Frati in *Atti e Mem. . . . Ferrara*, 1910, XX, I, p. 64 and A. Lazzarini, 'Il Barco di L. C.' in *Atti e Mem. . . . Ferrara*, 1919, XXIV, p. 12). Of the *Muses* nothing has remained. Belfiore was burned down in September 1483 and had to be rebuilt and re-decorated (documentary information on Belfiore in Venturi, 1888, p. 7f.).

1459

10. Tura makes three large and an unspecified number of small designs for tapestries and embroideries, to be used as bed-quilts, bench-covers and door-curtains on board a ship and in a palace: 'uno patrone grande da fare coperte da lecto e uno patrone da fare antiporti e uno da fare banchali de Razo'. The festivities to mark the arrival in Ferrara of Galeazzo Sforza are given as the reason for this order. Payment was made on 31 December (Venturi, 1885, p. 712, note 4).

11. *St. Peter and St. John the Baptist*. Philadelphia, Johnson Collection.   PLATES 3–4

12. *Madonna with the Zodiac Mandorla*. Rome, Principe Colonna.   PLATE 2

13. *St. George on horseback*. Manor House, Mells, Somerset (England), The Hon. Mrs. Kathanne Asquith.
                                              PLATE 6

1462

14. On the occasion of a tournament in honour of Prince Alberto Maria d'Este, Tura paints two tournament costumes and two large horse-trappings of taffeta 'che copre tuto lo cavallo sino in terra', the motives consisting of golden lilies, silver daisies and coloured ornaments; on a saddlecloth of red taffeta he also paints sieves with water running through them (probably one of Alberto's heraldic devices), coloured ornaments and

flowers. Payment was made on 6 August (Venturi, 1888, p. 8, note 5).

15. *Mercury* (drawing). Bayonne, Musée Bonnat.
                                              PLATE 7

16. *Christ* (or a Saint, or Marsyas) (drawing). Formerly Berlin, private collection.   PLATE 5

17. *Madonna with the sleeping Child*. Venice, Accademia.
                                              PLATE 8

18A. *Dancing children* (on a *Caritas* by another hand). Milan, Museo Poldi-Pezzoli.   PLATE V (Belongs to the same cycle as a *Prudentia* by Cossa and a *Spes* in which the knee-cloth has been repainted by Tura. Florence, Strozzi Collection; PLATE XIIB.)

18B. *Vesta standing by a candelabrum* (drawing, reworked). Vienna, Albertina.   PLATE VIIA

19. Altar-piece from Santa Maria della Consolazione, Ferrara. The centre panel is in the Musée Fesch at Ajaccio. Frame paintings in Rome, Principe Colonna; Milan, Museo Poldi-Pezzoli; Venice, Private Collection.
                                           PLATES 9–12

20. *Portrait of a Man*. Washington, National Gallery.
                                              PLATE 16

21. *Venus on a throne of dolphins*. London, National Gallery.   PLATES 14–15

22. *Caritas* (drawing). Berlin, Print Room (cf. No. *52*).
                                              PLATE 13

1464

23. In the Spring, for Alberto and Nicolò d'Este, Tura paints tournament equipment for horses and riders, viz. two horsecloths and three outer garments 'da homo', with ornaments in gold, silver and colours. Payments authorized on 7 March and 14 July (Venturi, 1885, p. 713, note 1).

24. By order of Duke Borso, Tura paints for Teofilo Calcagnini three pairs of leather horse-trappings, with ornaments in gold, ultramarine and other colours. Payment made to Tura on 25 February (Venturi, 1885, p. 713, note 2).

1465–7

25. Tura absent from Ferrara. According to Venturi (1885, p. 714f.) during these years he painted the library in the castle La Mirandola. Lelio Gregorio Giraldi (*Operum quae extant omnium*, Basilea, 1580, Vol. II) names Tura as the artist and states that the paintings consisted of panels in four parts with representations of allegories and the most celebrated poets (H. J. Hermann, *Jahrb. d. A. H. Kaiserhauses*, Vienna, 1898, p. 207f.). In addition there were crowns, armorial bearings and devices, and ornaments—the last-named probably in fresco—surrounding the pictures. Venturi quotes the following extract from Giraldi's dialogues: 'In one of the arch-spaces could be seen the figure of Poetry in the form of a venerable woman seated upon a chariot, richly attired, adorned with pearls and ear-rings, her countenance hidden by a flame-coloured veil; her expression was one of enthusiasm, in her right hand she held a tablet covered with various figures, in her left a globe and at her feet lay wreaths of laurel, ivy, myrtle and other foliage. In the picture beneath it would appear that the nine Muses were represented, dancing and offering crowns to singers, to whom Pytho, the goddess of persuasion, offered a clear liquid. The following pictures contained a half-length of Orpheus, his head covered by a tiara decorated with golden signs; an old man with the aspect of a peasant; Hesiod; and a portrait of Virgil, more godly in expression than all the other pictures. There were also representations of the Sibyls and lastly two women, sitting in chariots drawn by five horses, one of them grave and sad, the other gay and joyful, the former wearing a regal robe and mantle, the latter a white tunic; one holding in her hand a sceptre, the other a branch of myrtle. Both were surrounded by flute-players and singers while a multitude of poets and satyrs followed them' (1888, p. 11).

1467

26. After his return to Ferrara, probably in the autumn, Tura made further designs and coloured cartoons ('desegnato e depinto') for tapestries on two large pieces of canvas 'in the dimensions of a coverlet'. He also made sketches 'per fare fare panj de razj'. Payment was made to him on 31 December (Venturi, 1885, p. 712, note 5).

1467–8

27. Between the end of 1467 and 1468 Tura was commissioned by the brothers Uberto, Bartolomeo and Pietro Sacrati to decorate a chapel in San Domenico at Ferrara (Cittadella, 1868, II, p. 145). The walls were covered with frescoes showing scenes from the New Testament: 'intera storia del nuovo Testamento'. As altar-piece Tura painted an *Adoration of the Magi* (Baruffaldi, *Vite*, I, p. 67; M. A. Guarini, *Compend. Hist.*, Ferrara, 1621, p. 101). Payment for the whole of the work in the chapel was made to Tura at the end of 1468. The Sacrati chapel and the painting of the organ door

are the only two works by Tura that Vasari mentions (1550 edition, I, p. 428). In 1616 the frescoes were covered with whitewash (Guarini, p. 89) and when the church was transformed in 1717 they were lost. According to Baruffaldi the altar-piece was 'trasmutato' into a *St. Charles* by Ippolito Scarsellino (1551–1620). This picture now hangs in the fifth chapel on the left, on the front wall of which is a *Madonna* in fresco dating from the early part of the Quattrocento, but neither of these two works has anything to do with Tura.

28. St. Maurelius altar-piece from San Giorgio fuori le mura, Ferrara. Two portions in the Pinacoteca at Ferrara. PLATES 28–31

29. *The Madonna in the Garden* (above, The Annunciation). Washington, National Gallery.

PLATES 32–33

1468–9

30. Paintings on the organ-door of Ferrara Cathedral. Ferrara, Museo della Cattedrale. PLATES 17–27

1469–71

31. Supervision of the painting of the hall in Palazzo Schifanoia, Ferrara. PLATES 34–43

1469–72

32. Decoration of the chapel near the castle of Belriguardo near Voghiera. On 30 May 1469 a contract was made between Tura and Duke Borso, who wished to choose the subjects himself. The work, for which both Tura and two assistants were to be paid, was to be executed in five years, but as early as 31 March 1472 a valuation of it was made by Baldassare d'Este and Antonio Orsini. In July 1469 Tura went to Venice to buy colours and gold; at the beginning of November 1469 he was in Brescia, studying Gentile da Fabriano's paintings in the chapel of the episcopal palace ('la cappella de zentille'; cf. A. Ricci, *Memorie storice delle Arti . . . della Marca d'Ancona*, Macerata, 1834, I, p. 159 f.).

According to the 1472 report of the valuers, the Belriguardo chapel, built in 1469, evidently was a central dome with cruciform plan. Above the substructure was a tambour with eight semicircular windows and on top of this the main cupola. In addition to this there was a small cupola, perhaps the roofing of an apse, with six round windows.

The architraves, cornices, window-frames and other architectural components were decorated with stucco reliefs, the subjects being described as 145 'serafini' (heads of angels), animals, palm-leaves, branches of date-trees and foliage. These stucco reliefs were shaped, painted and gilded by Tura and his two assistants. An already existing terracotta frieze, made by 'muradori', was repaired ('recunzare') by them. In addition there were several actual paintings ('ad olio'), namely: a *God the Father* (probably in the small cupola) and eight half-lengths of *Evangelists* and *Fathers of the Church* ('octo mezi tondi'), which may have been on the walls of the tambour between the eight semicircular windows. These nine figures were enframed in elaborate, partially sculptured niches.

According to Venturi (*Cosmè Tura e la Cappella di Belriguardo, Il Buonarroti,* 1885, p. 3 f.), the chapel stood apart from the great complex of castle buildings grouped around two square courts. In the sixteenth century Alfonso II had sweeping changes made and there were further alterations during the Baroque period and in the nineteenth century. Nothing now remains of the Tura chapel.

1471

33. Tura is paid 20 lire for decorating the catafalque of Duke Borso, who died on 19 August (cf. A. Neppi, *Tura,* 1952, p. 35).

34. Madonna with Saints Sebastian, Francis, Dominic and Agatha (drawing). London, British Museum.

PLATE 44

35. St. John on Patmos. Genoa, collection of Sig. G. B. Gnecco.   PLATE 45

36. Christ on the Cross with the Virgin Mary and St. John. Cambridge, Fitzwilliam Museum.   PLATE 49

37. The Lamentation (tapestry after a design by Tura). Copies in the Neven-Dumont collection, Cologne, and in the Museum of Art, Cleveland (Ohio).

PLATES IIC, IIIC

38. A Father (or *Doctor*) *of the Church* (drawing; also attributed to Giovanni Bellini). Bayonne, Musée Bonnat.

PLATE XC

39. Pietà (painted terracotta; also attributed to Domenico di Paris). Formerly in the Ventura collection, Florence.

PLATE 46

1472 (?)

40A. Pietà. Venice, Museo Civico Correr.

PLATES 47–8

40B. Pietà (drawing, reworked by another hand). London, Mrs. M. H. Drey.   PLATE IX

1472

41. Some time in the late summer or early autumn Tura made a coloured sketch for the decoration of the canopy of the bridal bed of Duke Ercole and Eleonora d'Aragona; it consisted of embroidery in wool and silk on a white ground and was executed by Giovanni Mille and Rubinetto di Francia (Venturi, 1890, p. 36, note 2).

1472

42. At the end of the year Tura made a portrait ('testa' on canvas) of Duke Ercole I. The portrait was to be sent to Naples as a gift for Ercole's betrothed, Eleonora d'Aragona (Venturi, 1888, p. 21, note 1).

1472

43. Portrait of Princess Lucrezia d'Este (as above, No. 42).

1472–3

44. Designs by Tura for a silver table service. Tura went to Venice to discuss the matter with the goldsmith Giorgio Alegretto da Ragusa, who was to execute his designs. According to an inventory of the Guardaroba made on 22 October 1473 the table service consisted of: 1. Three large flasks, each with two 'wild men' as supporters (these six 'homini salvatici' were melted down in April 1474 and Pietro da Milano made from the material a new vessel after an already existing design by Amadio da Milano): 'They were large flasks with their necks rising from amidst the heads and talons of griffins, with satyrs rising out of the griffins' legs and supporting the bodies of the flasks in the manner of caryatids' (Venturi, 1888, p. 22). 2. A large pitcher with a lid crowned with the plastic representation of an Estensian emblem, all gilded. This was a counterpart to an already existing older piece. 3. Another counterpart; a twin-handled pitcher with lid, with decorations in relief; partially gilded. 4. Two large, partially gilded vessels with lids, each adorned with four putti on the lid, and Estensian crests and devices in relief and painted enamel on the neck, body and base. 5. Two partially gilded vessels with lids and artistically decorated bases; on the other parts of each vessel four Estensian emblems, each flanked by two putti blowing trumpets. The decorations were in relief and niello. 6. Two partially gilded vessels with decorations in relief and enamel, consisting of devices of Duke Ercole with a putto, and handles formed of eagles. 7. Two similar vessels decorated with devices, each with two cornucopiae full of flowers in painted enamel. 8. Two similar vessels adorned with garlands 'alantiqua', each with two dolphins as handles. 9. Two partially gilded flasks with handles, with decorations in relief, niello and painted enamel. 10. Two silver-gilt flasks with lids, with the ducal coat of arms in relief and enamel. 11. Eleven large beakers, carved in relief and chased, with animals and foliage. 12. Six similarly adorned bowls, with, in addition, the ducal coat of arms (Venturi, 1888, p. 22f., note 3). Cf. *No. 64*.

1473-4

45. Tura makes drawings for silver embroideries on horsecloths and for other purposes ('piu altre raxon'), which Amadio da Milano was to execute (Venturi, 1890, p. 38f., note 1).

1474

46. On 12 November Tura receives payment for two large and two small tapestry designs on canvas for chair-backs. Also for two sets of drawings for door-curtains and coverings for benches and other furniture. The subjects were Estensian coats of arms amidst decorations of foliage and animals. By 1475 these had been woven by Giovanni Costa, Giovanni Mille and Giovanni da Correggio (Campori, 1876, p. 27).

47. Portions of the predella of an altar-piece (assumed by Longhi to be the Roverella altar-piece). Cambridge, Mass., Fogg Art Museum; Boston, Mass., Gardner Museum; New York, Metropolitan Museum.

PLATES 60-3

1474

48. Roverella altar-piece for San Giorgio fuori le mura, Ferrara. Centre panel in London, National Gallery. Wings in Rome, Principe Colonna collection, and San Diego, Fine Arts Gallery. Lunette in Paris, Louvre.

FRONTISPIECE AND PLATES 50-9

1475

49. On 18 April Tura received payment for 'piu designj facti in piu volte adi passati per Raci' (Venturi, 1890, p. 40, note 5). Between 1475 and 1483 Rubinetto di Francia is said to have woven after Tura's designs an altar-cloth, a 'palio d'altare', and other articles (Campori, 1876, p. 24f.).

1475

50. Small domestic altar-piece for Duke Ercole I. From this probably come the four little panels: *The Annunciation with Saints Francis and Maurelius*. Washington, National Gallery.

PLATES 64-7

1477

51. Tura is commissioned to make three portraits ('tre Imazini naturale', Venturi, 1890, p. 42, note 2) of the one-year-old Don Alfonso d'Este. The first of these was finished on 27 July and Tura worked on the other two

until October. At the beginning of the seventeenth century one of the portraits of Alfonso was probably in the Canonici collection at Ferrara—attributed to 'Lorenzo Costa' (C. Padovani, *La Critica d'Arte e la Pittura Ferrarese*, Rovigo, 1954, p. 132f.). Towards the end of that century it was in the possession of the father of G. Baruffaldi, who describes it as 'un tal ritratto esemplare di tutti, sicchè ancora dopo molti anni appare egli bello, vivace, parlante' (*Vite*, I, p. 108). No trace of it now remains. (A miniature portrait of Eleonora d'Aragon, in a Ferrarese manuscript of about 1475-80— now Pierpont Morgan Library MS. 731—was attributed by Berenson to Tura himself.)

1477-81

52. Tura executes works for Duke Ercole I's studio. Four already existing panels 'ad olio' had only to be altered or repaired, and three new ones had to be painted. The subjects were nude allegorical female figures, the meaning of which is not stated. As they were seven in number, they may have been *Virtues*; the *Caritas* of drawing No. 22 (Plate 13) is a nude female figure symbolizing a Virtue. As the Allegories already existing in the studio may have been earlier works of Tura's, it is also possible that this *Caritas* was a preliminary sketch for one of the Allegories in Ercole I's studio. In September 1471 Tura was given supplies of gold and blue, and again in February 1481. The first two payments were made in March and August 1481 and on 6 May 1483 he demanded the last payment (for these and other paintings) (Venturi, 1888, p. 26f., note 4).

53. Altar-piece (said to come from the Certosa in Ferrara): *St. Jerome in Penitence*. Main part in London, National Gallery; a fragment in Milan, Brera.

PLATES 68-9

54. *Hercules and the lion* (drawing). Rotterdam, Boymans Museum.

PLATE 70

1479

55. Portrait 'ad Naturalem' of Princess Lucrezia d'Este (commissioned by the Duchess Eleonora) as 'Sponse promisse Magnifico D. Hanibali De Bentivolys'. Instructions for the payment were given on 28 January (Venturi, 1890, p. 45, note 1).

1479

56. In the autumn Tura makes two drawings for a door-curtain, to be woven by Giovanni Mille, and for a mule-cloth, to be executed in several copies by Rinaldo di Bretagna. Payment to Tura was made on 10 December (Venturi, 1888, p. 28, note 3).

1480

57. In the Spring Tura paints a wedding portrait of Isabella d'Este ('testa'). Payment was made to him on 30 March 1480 (Venturi, 1888, p. 28, note 2).

1480

58. Design for a carpet to be executed by Rubinetto di Francia, showing the *Judgement of Solomon* (? 'instoria de Salamone'). Payment made to Tura on 31 December (Venturi, 1890, p. 46, note 3).

59. An Evangelist reading (drawing). Florence, Uffizi, Gabinetto dei Disegni.　　　　PLATE 71

1484 (?)

60. Polyptych A, said to have come from San Luca in Borgo, Ferrara. Two portions in Berlin, former Staatl. Museen.　　　　PLATES 72–4

1484 (?)

61. Polyptych B. Three parts in Caen, Musée Mancel; Paris, Louvre; Florence, Uffizi.　　　　PLATES 75–7

62. Polyptych C, perhaps from San Giacomo, Argenta. Centre panel in Bergamo, Accademia Carrara. Side-panels in New York, Metropolitan Museum, and Nantes, Musée Municipal. Lunette in Vienna, Kunsthistorisches Museum.　　　　PLATES 78–82

1484

63. Altar-piece from San Nicolò, Ferrara: *St. Anthony of Padua*. Modena, Galleria Estense.　　　　PLATES 83–5

1485

64. In 1483 Lodovico il Moro had already asked Duke Ercole d'Este to lend him Tura's designs for the ducal table service (Venturi, 'Relazioni artistiche tra le corti di Milano e Ferrara', *Archivio Storico Lomb.*, Milan, 1885, II, p. 2). In 1485 a drawing by Tura was sent to Lodovico: 'uno desegno de la credenza cum le arezentarie de sala grande de sua ex.ᵃ'. Even if there was some connection with Tura's designs for a table-service made in 1472–3 (*No. 44*; cf. Campori, 1886, p. 37f.), the wording of the document makes it probable that in this case Tura made a new drawing showing all the articles of the service on one sheet.

1485

65. Bust-length portrait of the fifteen-year-old Princess Beatrice d'Este as bride of Lodovico il Moro (Venturi, 1888, p. 28f., note 6).

66. Virgin of the Annunciation, fragment (workshop production; only small portions by Tura's own hand). London, National Gallery.　　　　PLATE IV

1493

67. The astronomer Alfraganus and the mathematician Eremita da Padova. Woodcut, probably after a drawing by Tura. Illustration for *Alfragani compilatio astronomica*, Ferrara, 1493, fol. 1 v.　　　　Reproduced below.

Alfraganus and Eremita. Woodcut, Ferrara, 1493, after a drawing by Tura(?).

PLATES

I. PORTRAIT OF A MEMBER OF THE ESTE FAMILY. *New York, Metropolitan Museum*

2. MADONNA WITH ZODIAC MANDORLA. *Rome, Principe Colonna*

3-4. SAINT PETER AND SAINT JOHN THE BAPTIST. *Philadelphia, John G. Johnson Collection*

5. CHRIST (?) AT THE COLUMN. Pen drawing.
Formerly Berlin, Private Collection

6. SAINT GEORGE AND THE DRAGON. *Mells, Frome, Somerset, Hon. Mrs. K. Asquith*

7. MERCURY AS PLANETARY DIVINITY. Pen drawing. *Bayonne, Musée Bonnat*

8. MADONNA WITH SLEEPING CHILD . *Venice, Academy*

9. VIRGIN OF THE ANNUNCIATION. (Belonging to Plate 12.)
Rome, Principe Colonna

10. SAINT MAURELIUS (?). (Belonging to Plate 12.) *Milan, Museo Poldi Pezzoli*

11. SAINT GEORGE AND THE DRAGON. (Belonging to Plate 12.)
Venice, Private Collection

12. MADONNA BETWEEN SAINTS JEROME AND APOLLONIA. Altar-piece from S. Maria della Consolazione. *Ajaccio, Musée Fesch*

13. CHARITY. Drawing. *Berlin, Print Room*

14. ALLEGORICAL FIGURE (VENUS). *London, National Gallery*

15. ALLEGORICAL FIGURE. Detail from Plate 14

16. PORTRAIT OF A MAN. *Washington, National Gallery of Art (Samuel H. Kress Collection)*

17. SAINT GEORGE KILLING THE DRAGON. Left wing of an organ-door.
Ferrara, Museo della Cattedrale. 1468-9.

18. SAINT GEORGE KILLING THE DRAGON. Right wing of an organ-door.
Ferrara, Museo della Cattedrale. 1468-9.

19. THE ANGEL OF THE ANNUNCIATION. Left wing of an organ-door.
Ferrara, Museo della Cattedrale

20. THE VIRGIN OF THE ANNUNCIATION. Right wing of an organ-door.
Ferrara, Museo della Cattedrale

21. THE PRINCESS. Detail from Plate 17

22. SAINT GEORGE. Detail from Plate 18

23. GABRIEL. Detail from Plate 19

24. DECORATED ARCH. Detail from Plate 20

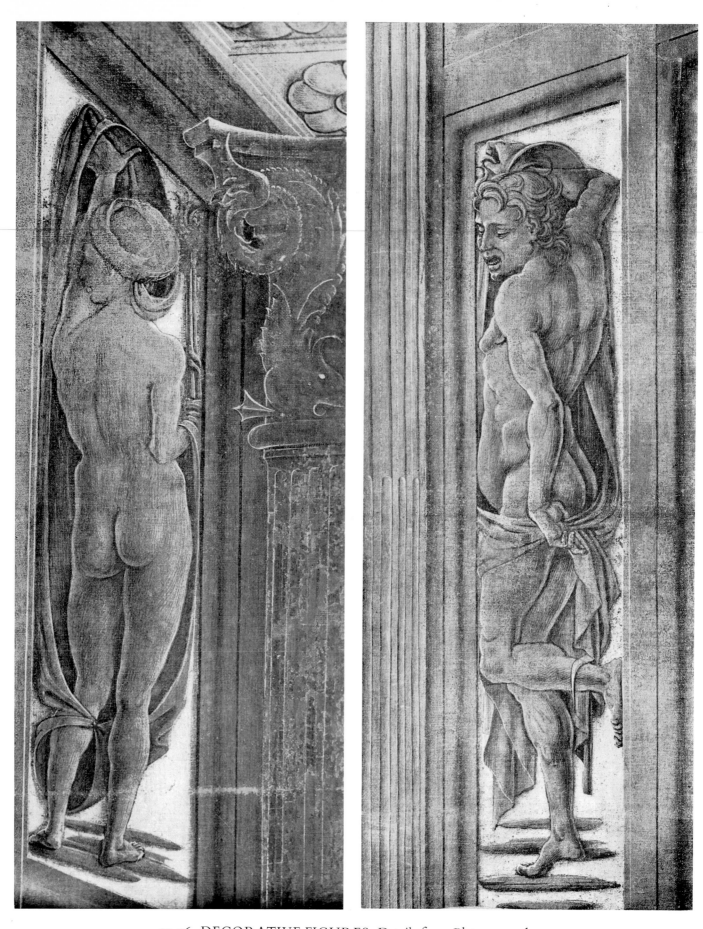

25-26. DECORATIVE FIGURES. Details from Plates 19 and 20

27. DECORATIVE FIGURES. Detail from Plate 20

28. THE CONDEMNATION OF SAINT MAURELIUS. From the Maurelius altar-piece.
Ferrara, Pinacoteca

29. THE EXECUTION OF SAINT MAURELIUS. From the Maurelius altar-piece.
Ferrara, Pinacoteca

30. THE JUDGE. Detail from Plate 28

31. STANDARD-BEARER AND EXECUTIONER. Detail from Plate 29

32. MADONNA IN A GARDEN; above, THE ANNUNCIATION.
Washington, National Gallery of Art (Samuel H. Kress Collection)

33. THE VIRGIN OF THE ANNUNCIATION. Detail from Plate 32 (enlarged to twice original size)

34. SEPTEMBER. Fresco. *Ferrara, Palazzo Schifanoia.* 1469-71.

35. VULCAN'S FORGE. Detail from Plate 34

36. VULCAN. Detail from Plate 34

37. THE ROMAN SHE-WOLF. Detail from Plate 34

38. LANDSCAPE WITH EROTES. Detail from Plate 34

39. MARS AND VENUS. Detail from Plate 34

40. ASTROLOGICAL DEMON: THE NINETEENTH DECAN. Detail from Plate 34

41. ASTROLOGICAL DEMONS: THE TWENTY-FIRST DECAN. Detail from Plate 34

42. THE ENTOURAGE OF THE DUKE OF FERRARA. Detail from Plate 34

43. THE VIRGO OF THE ZODIAC AND AN ASTROLOGICAL DEMON. *Fresco, centre part. Ferrara, Palazzo Schifanoia. 1469–71.*

44. MADONNA BETWEEN SAINTS SEBASTIAN, FRANCIS, DOMINIC AND AGATHA.
Pen drawing. *London, British Museum*

45. SAINT JOHN ON PATMOS. *Genoa, Gnecco Collection*

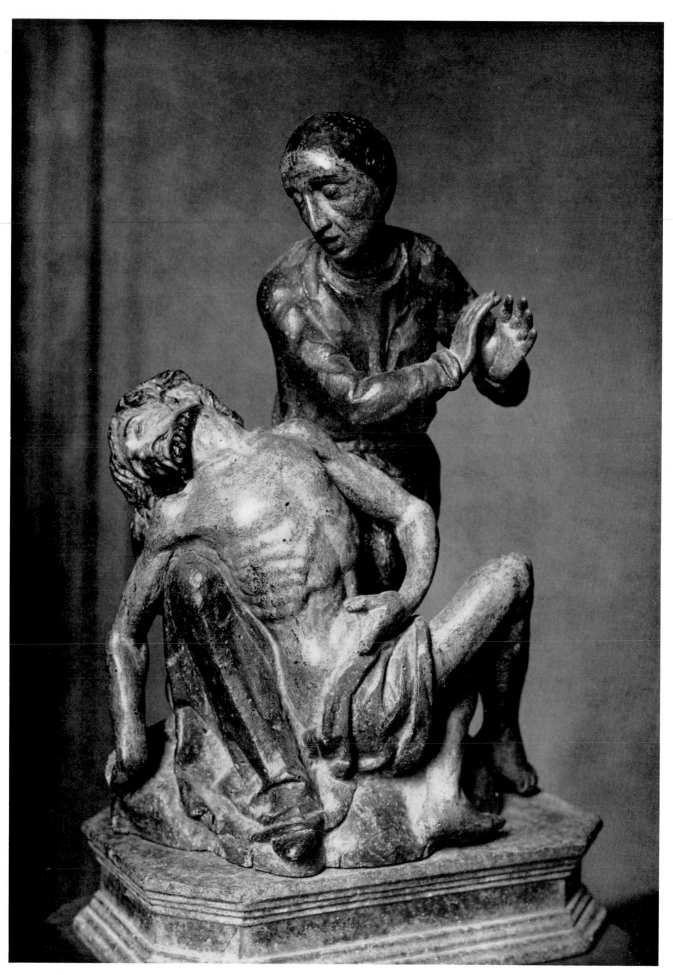

46. PIETÀ. Painted terracotta. *Formerly Florence, Ventura Collection*

47. PIETÀ. *Venice, Museo Civico Correr.* 1472 (?)

48. THE THREE CROSSES. Detail from Plate 47

49. CHRIST ON THE CROSS WITH THE VIRGIN AND SAINT JOHN.
Cambridge, Fitzwilliam Museum

50. MADONNA AND ANGELS MAKING MUSIC.
From the Roverella altar-piece. *London, National Gallery.* 1474 (?)

51. SAINTS PAUL AND MAURELIUS WITH (?) NICOLO ROVERELLA.
From the Roverella altar-piece. *Rome, Principe Colonna.* 1474 (?)

52. SAINT GEORGE. From the Roverella altar-piece. *San Diego (California), Fine Arts Gallery.* 1474 (?)

53. DECORATIONS ON THE CANOPY OF THE THRONE. Detail from Plate 50

54. ANGEL MUSICIANS. Detail from Plate 50

55. ANGEL MUSICIANS. Detail from Plate 50

56. TWO ANGELS. Detail from Plate 50

57. THE LAMENTATION. From the Roverella altar-piece. *Paris, Louvre.* 1474 (?)

58. TWO SAINTS. Detail from Plate 57

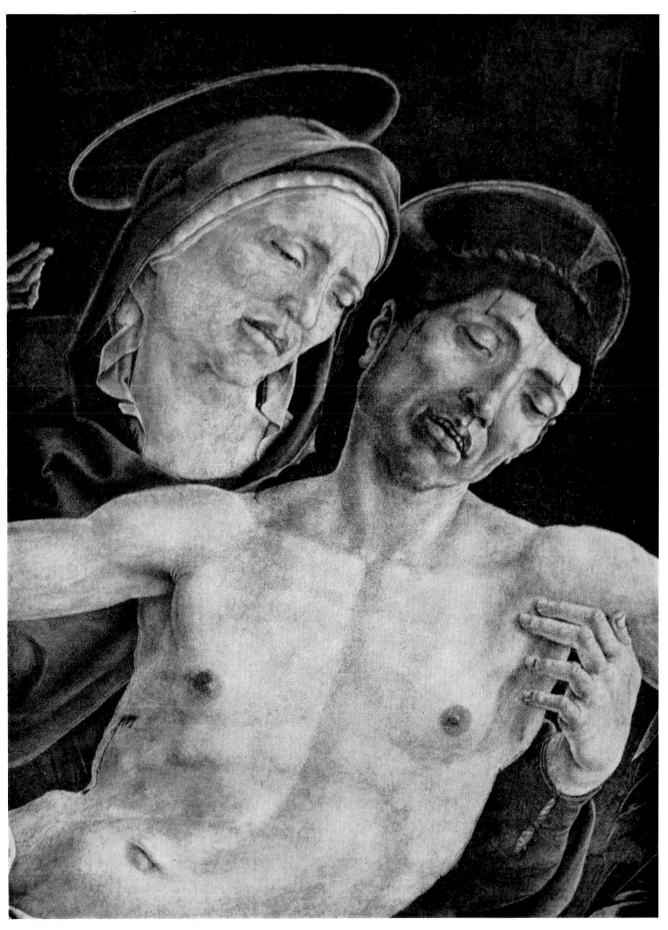

59. CHRIST AND THE VIRGIN. Detail from Plate 57

60. THE CIRCUMCISION. (From the same predella as Plates 62 and 63.)
Boston, Isabella Stewart Gardner Museum

61. SIMEON AND ANNA. Detail from Plate 60

62. THE ADORATION OF THE MAGI. (From the same predella as Plates 60 and 63.)
Cambridge (Mass.), Fogg Art Museum

63. THE FLIGHT INTO EGYPT. (From the same predella as Plates 60 and 62.)
New York, Metropolitan Museum

64-65. THE ANNUNCIATION. (From the same dismembered polyptych as Plates 66-67.)
Washington, National Gallery of Art (Samuel H. Kress Collection). 1475 (?)

66-67. SAINTS FRANCIS AND MAURELIUS. (From the same dismembered polyptych as Plates 64-65.)
Washington, National Gallery of Art (Samuel H. Kress Collection). 1475 (?)

68. CRUCIFIX. Fragment. (Belonging to Plate 69. Reproduced in original size.) *Milan, Brera*

69. SAINT JEROME IN PENITENCE. Fragment. *London, National Gallery*

70. HERCULES AND THE LION. Brush drawing. *Rotterdam, Museum Boymans*

71. AN EVANGELIST READING. Brush drawing. *Florence, Uffizi, Print Room*

72. SAINT CHRISTOPHER. (From the same set as Plate 74.)
Berlin, Kaiser Friedrich Museum. 1484 (?)

73. THE CHRIST CHILD AND SAINT CHRISTOPHER. Detail from Plate 72

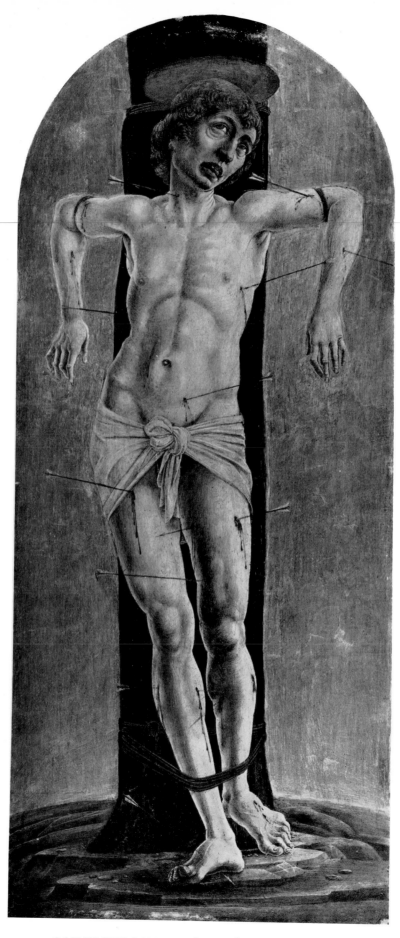

74. SAINT SEBASTIAN. (From the same set as Plate 72.)
Berlin, Kaiser Friedrich Museum. 1484 (?)

75. SAINT JAMES MAJOR. (From the same set as Plates 76 and 77.)
Caen, Musée des Beaux-Arts. 1484 (?)

76. SAINT ANTHONY OF PADUA. (From the same set as Plates 75 and 77.)
Paris, Louvre. 1484 (?)

77. **SAINT DOMINIC**. Fragment. (From the same set as Plates 75 and 76.) *Florence, Uffizi.* 1484 (?)

78. SAINT LOUIS OF TOULOUSE.
New York, Metropolitan Museum

79. SAINT NICHOLAS OF BARI.
Nantes, Musée municipal

(From the same polyptych as Plates 80 and 81.)

80. MADONNA WITH BLESSING CHILD. (From the same polyptych as Plates 78, 79, 81.)
Bergamo, Accademia Carrara

81. DEAD CHRIST SUPPORTED BY TWO ANGELS. (From the same polyptych as Plates 78–80.) *Vienna, Kunsthistorisches Museum*

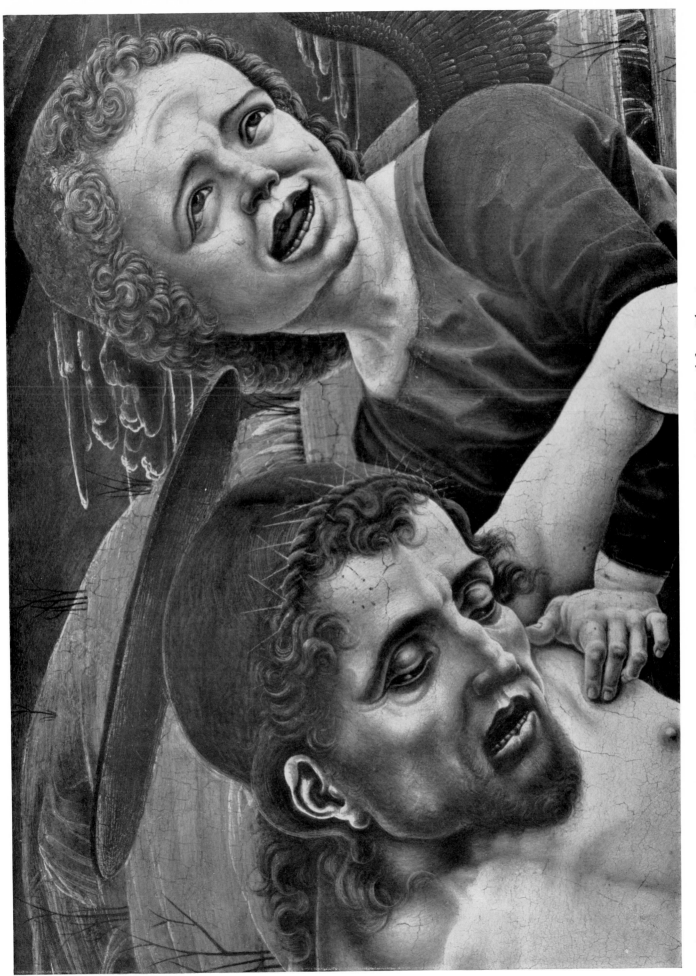

82. CHRIST AND A MOURNING ANGEL. Detail from Plate 81

83. SAINT ANTHONY OF PADUA. *Modena, Galleria Estense*. 1484 (?)

84. SAINT ANTHONY OF PADUA. Detail from Plate 83

85. LANDSCAPE. Detail from Plate 83

NOTES ON THE PLATES

NOTES ON THE PLATES

1. PORTRAIT OF A YOUNG PRINCE OF THE HOUSE OF ESTE. New York, Metropolitan Museum (14.40.649).

On wood; 11⅞ × 8½ inches (30·2 × 21·6 cm.).

The subject is about fifteen years old and has Estensian features, for which reason it was formerly believed that this was a portrait of Borso d'Este as a boy. Borso, however, was born in 1413, and as the picture cannot have been painted before 1450, it cannot be a portrait of him. The portrait of a 'nobile giovinetto' has evidently always been attributed to Tura (C. Laderchi, *Quadreria Costabili*, 1838, I, p. 28).

R. Longhi (*Officina Ferrarese*, 1934, pp. 74, 171) dates it about 1460–5, but as it is the most austere and antiquated work by Tura that we know, and as it obviously has some connection with a number of portraits of other Estensian princes painted about 1450 (see pp. 9, 13f. above), it must be assigned to the early days of Tura's activity for the Court, which we know began in 1451. In 1838 the 'nobile giovinetto' was No. 22 in the Costabili collection, Ferrara (see above). Later it passed to W. Drury Lowe, Locko Park, and then to Benjamin Altman, New York. Since 1913 it has been in the Metropolitan Museum.

Further bibliography: G. Fiocco, *Pantheon*, 1932, p. 338; B. Berenson, *Pitture italiane*, Milan, 1936, p. 500; *Catalogue of the Metropolitan Museum*, 1940, p. 130; *Metropolitan Museum Bulletin*, November 1944.

2. MADONNA WITH THE ZODIAC MANDORLA. Rome, Principe Colonna.

On wood; 8¼ × 5⅛ inches (21 × 13 cm.).

On the mandorla behind the Virgin are symbols of the Zodiac: Taurus, Gemini, Cancer, Leo, Virgo (?), Libra (?), Scorpio, Sagittarius, Capricornus (symbolized by the Estensian unicorn).

As it has the same dimensions, this little picture is generally supposed to be connected with the small paintings reproduced in Plates 9–11, which formed part of the altar-piece in Santa Maria della Consolazione. The latter, however, was itself a *Madonna* altar-piece and the modelling, technique and linear ductus of the pictures shown in Plates 9–11 are far freer than is the case

with the Roman *Madonna*, so that the connection seems doubtful. In its degree of stylistic development the Roman *Madonna* is closer to the Saints of Plates 3 and 4 and, like these, may be dated about 1460.

The provenance of the picture is difficult to establish, since Tura *Madonnas* are mentioned very frequently in the chronicles and old catalogues. The Colonna collection has been in possession of works by Tura since 1836.

3–4. ST. PETER AND ST. JOHN THE BAPTIST. Philadelphia, John G. Johnson Collection (241).

On wood; each panel 8¼ × 4¼ inches (21 × 10·8 cm.) without frame.

Attributed to Tura by A. Venturi (*Storia dell'Arte*, 1914, VII, III, p. 546); R. Longhi believes it to be a workshop production (*Officina Ferrarese*, 1934, p. 161), but this seems hardly necessary if it is properly dated.

Venturi (see above) suggests the middle of the 1470's as the date of execution, but the Late Gothic carving of the frame, the austerity of the linear ductus and the constrained calligraphy point to a considerably earlier date —about 1460. All subsequent pictures give the impression of being far more developed.

In 1888 the panels were in the Panciatichi gallery, Florence (O. Härtzsch, *Tura-Katalog*, 1931, p. 23).

Further bibliography: *Catalogues of the Johnson Collection*, 1931, p. 153f. and 1941, p. 16.

5. CHRIST (?) AT THE COLUMN. Formerly Berlin, private collection.

Pen-drawing; 8⅞ × 5¾ inches (22·5 × 14·5 cm.).

The figure has a certain resemblance to the destroyed *Christopher* by Mantegna from the martyrdom fresco in the Ovetari chapel at Padua (cf. the copy in F. Knapp, *Mantegna*, Stuttgart-Leipzig, 1910, p. xxii). In the Hollstein and Puppel auction catalogue, Berlin, October–November 1929, No. 101, this drawing is described as 'close to Mantegna', but R. Longhi recognized it as a work of Tura's (*Ampliamenti nell'Officina Ferrarese, Supplemento all'anno IV de 'La Critica d'Arte'*, Florence, 1940, p. 5). L. Goldscheider, in a letter to me, suggests that the figure represents a Marsyas (cf. also Plate 26).

The identity of style and similarity in size with the *Mercury* (Plate 7)—whom Greek mythology regards as the father of all satyrs—strengthens this interpretation. Thus both drawings could be linked with the programme for the studio of Belfiore, and might, in fact, be the only traces left of it.

Longhi's dating 'about 1470' seems doubtful if we compare the drawing with the 'reliefs' in the paintings on the organ door, Plates 25–7, completed in 1469; around 1470 Tura used a different style for his folds. It is more likely that this and the following drawing, Plate 7, were made about 1460 like the pictures reproduced in Plates 2–4 and 8–12.

6. ST. GEORGE AND THE DRAGON. The Hon. Mrs. Kathanne Asquith, Manor House, Mells, Frome, Somerset (England).

On wood; $14\frac{1}{2} \times 7\frac{1}{4}$ inches ($34\cdot3 \times 18\cdot4$ cm.). With lateral additions $8\frac{1}{2}$ inches ($21\cdot6$ cm.) wide.

My attention was drawn to this picture (permission for the reproduction of which for the first time has been kindly granted by the owner) by Ludwig Goldscheider. A comparison with Tura's representations of St. George in Venice (Plate 11) and Ferrara (Plate 18) provides convincing proof of the correctness of this attribution. The invention as a whole is significant and reveals that expressive leaning towards the unusual so characteristic of Tura—the jagged, upward swirl of the dragon's limbs gives the impression that the Saint is riding through flames. Later, in his *St. Michael* towering above Satan writhing on the ground, now in the Louvre, Ercole Roberti tried to realize a similar conception.

Stylistically, the painting is in the immediate neighbourhood of the small panels in Philadelphia (Plates 3–4); particularly noteworthy are the tranquil expression, the firm modelling, the brittle pictorial calligraphy and the style of the folds. There is also a certain artlessness in the choice of the proportions—the over-large dimensions of the Saint in comparison with the animals—which points to the picture having been painted about 1460.

According to a letter received from the owner (1957), the picture has been in the possession of her family for a long time; her grandfather, the art-collector William Graham, bequeathed it to her mother Lady Horner, who in turn left it to the present owner.

7. MERCURY AS A PLANETARY DIVINITY. Bayonne, Musée Bonnat.

Pen-drawing; $9\frac{1}{2} \times 6\frac{3}{4}$ inches (24×17 cm.).

K. T. Parker, in *North Italian Drawings*, London, 1927, pp. 13, 28, attributes this drawing to Ercole Roberti.

Nevertheless, a comparison with the drawing in Plate 5, obviously by the same hand, shows that Roberti, whose style of drawing is known from a number of more or less certain attributions, can hardly have been the author of these two drawings. In the attitude and movement of the figure, in the treatment of the body and in style, the *Mercury* is very close to the *St. George* of Plate 11, which is undoubtedly by Tura.

As regards the dating—about 1460—see note to Plate 5.

8. MADONNA WITH SLEEPING CHILD. Venice, Accademia (628).

On wood; $46\frac{7}{8} \times 23\frac{1}{4}$ inches (including frame) (119×59 cm.). See Plate I.

On the parapet the inscription: SVIGLIA EL TVO FIGLIO DOLCE MADRE PIA/PER FAR IN FIN FELICE LALMA MIA. Behind the Virgin the signs of the Zodiac, in gold, from Virgo to Aquarius. In the lunette, two angels with symbols of St. Bernard. See Plate IIA.

As regards the date of this altar-piece, the authenticity of which has never been disputed, there is hardly any positive evidence. The style of the folds in the dress and mantle has the constraint of the early works (cf. Plates 2–7); on the other hand, there are certain Netherlandish elements (type of the Madonna, style of the head-dress, draughtsmanship of the hands). In the general conception, however, there is a highly developed assuredness, so that one is tempted to consider the altar-piece as one of the last of the early works executed about 1460.

The picture was formerly in the Casa Filippo Bertoldi at Merlara near Montagnana. In 1896 it was purchased from a subsequent owner by the Accademia. Restored in 1896–7 by G. Spoldi and in 1938 by Pellicioli (cf. S. Moschini-Marconi, *Galleria dell'Accademia*, Rome, 1955, p. 179f.).

9–12. ALTAR-PIECE FROM SANTA MARIA DELLA CONSOLAZIONE

9. *The Virgin of the Annunciation.* Rome, Principe Colonna.

On wood; $8\frac{1}{4} \times 4\frac{3}{4}$ inches (21×12 cm.).

10. *A Bishop-Saint* (Maurelius?). Milan, Museo Poldi-Pezzoli (600).

On wood; $8\frac{1}{4} \times 4\frac{3}{4}$ inches (21×12 cm.).

11. *St. George and the Dragon.* Venice, private collection.

On wood, $8\frac{1}{2} \times 5\frac{1}{8}$ ($21\cdot6 \times 13$ cm.).

The above paintings were on the frame of:

12. *Madonna with Saints Jerome and Apollonia.* Ajaccio (Corsica), Musée Fesch (127).

Canvas (on wood); 59⅞ × 39¾ inches (152 × 101 cm.).

In the main picture, on the front of the step, the inscription ANTONIO CICOGNARA VERGINE PVRA/ DIPINGER FECE QVESTA TVA FIGVRA. That the three little panels on wood and the painting on canvas formed part of the same altar-piece is proved by analogies of style, colouring and motive; the motive of the pillar is the same in all four. The wood panels must have adorned the frame of the large painting on canvas. There must also have been other portions, now lost; certainly a small *Angel of the Annunciation*, and perhaps a semi-circular lunette picture. In the sacristy of Santa Maria della Consolazione, whence the altar-piece came, C. Cittadella (*Cat. Ist.*, 1782-3, I, p. 52) saw a 'Pietà con mezze figure', allegedly by Tura. In the eighteenth century the main picture was attributed to Baldassare d'Este (C. Barotti, *Pitt. e Scult.*, Ferrara, 1770, p. 167; G. Scalabrini, *Chiese di Ferrara*, 1773, p. 236). In 1834, when in the Pasini collection, Rome, it was thought to be by Francesco del Cossa. Despite the words in the inscription 'dipinger *fece*', Bernard Berenson first attributed it to the painter Antonio Cicognara, who had the same name as the man who commissioned the work (1932, p. 144), and later (1936, p. 499) described it as a workshop production. R. Longhi, however, recognized it as a work by Tura's own hand (*Officina Ferrarese*, Rome, 1934, pp. 35f., 160).

Longhi called the main picture a late work by Tura, but admitted verbally on 6 October 1956 that it might be a fairly early work, which is confirmed by the present impression after the picture had been cleaned and exhibited in Paris in 1956 (M. Laclotte, *Catalogue De Giotto à Bellini*, Paris, 1956, p. 87f.). The picture is in close relationship as regards style and atmosphere to the early works shown in Plates 1-8, but at the same time already has points of contact with the London *Venus* (Plates 14, 15) and the portrait reproduced in Plate 16. Side by side with antiquated details—especially in the *St. George*—we find an extremely new form of calligraphy, which in the *St. Maurelius* is almost sketchy. That such sketch-like portions, which are found again and again in Tura's works, had a completely different character in the later works, is shown by a comparison with Plates 49, 60-1, 70, 71, 73. But above all the rigid ornamental style of the folds in Tura's last works is so fundamentally different from the temperamental agitation of the folds in the Consolazione altar-piece, that we are bound to assume that a considerable interval elapsed

between the execution of the former and the latter. This altar-piece, too, must be dated at the beginning of the 1460's.

The fact that the altar-piece came from the Ferrarese church of Santa Maria della Consolazione is confirmed by Barotti, Scalabrini (see above), G. Boschini and others (cf. also Venturi, *Storia dell'Arte*, 1914, VII, III p. 616f., and Laclotte, *op. cit.*, p. 87f.). It is expressly stated that it consisted of 'Maria Vergine, e diversi Santi, con altre pitture'; in other words that the *Madonna* painting was not the only one in the sacristy. The main picture subsequently passed to the private collections of Sacchetti (1770; cf. Padovani, *La Critica d'Arte*, Rovigo, 1954, p. 140), U. Sgherbi, G. Saroli (Padovani, p. 160) —all in Ferrara—F. Pasini, Rome (1834), and Cardinal Fesch, whence in 1839 it went to the museum in Ajaccio (catalogue 1892, No. 127).

In 1838 the little frame pictures were Nos. 23 and 24 and perhaps also No. 20 in the Costabili collection, Ferrara. A *St. George*, evidently a small one, allegedly by Tura, was seen in 1782 by C. Cittadella in the F. Rizzoni collection, Ferrara (*Cat. Ist.*, II, p. 212). In 1874 there was a little *St. George* by Tura in the collection of Countess Biella, Venice (Crowe & Cavalcaselle, V, II, p. 554). From the Earl of Rosebery's collection (Leighton Buzzard, England) the *St. George* of Plate 11 came on to the New York market (December 1946), and thence passed to the present owner; the *Bishop-Saint* of Plate 10 was acquired in 1885 for the Poldi-Pezzoli collection, Milan (F. Russoli, Catalogue 1955, p. 223f.). There is a later, free workshop variant of the *Madonna of the Annunciation* in the National Gallery, London (905); see Plate IV.

13. CARITAS. Berlin, Print Room (5051).

Brush-drawing, heightened with white; 9¼ × 5⅜ inches (24.3 × 13.5 cm.).

Perhaps a study for a cycle of nude allegorical female figures on which Tura resumed work in 1477 in Duke Ercole I's studio (cf. the Chronological List of Works, No. 52).

This drawing was first made known as a work of Tura's by F. von Harck (*Jahrbuch der Preussischen Kunstsammlungen*, 1884, V, p. 120, note).

Stylistically it is very close to the London *Venus* (cf. Plate 14), the paintings on the organ door (cf. Plates 17 and 19), the *St. Maurelius* altar-piece (cf. Plate 30) and the frescoes in Palazzo Schifanoia (cf. especially Plate 36), works, that is to say, which for the most part were painted after the middle 1460's. The drawing is dated about 1466 by S. Ortolani, who relates it to the allegories in La Mirandola (cf. Chronological List, No. 25), though as regards subject it is difficult to fit it into the programme of these. This drawing, together with the whole cycle of allegories for the studio, was probably planned before Tura left for La Mirandola, and his departure would thus explain the interruption of the work on the cycle.

Purchased in 1902 from the von Beckerath collection (*Handzeichnungen alter Meister im Kupferstichkabinett, Berlin*, 1910, No. 45).

14–15. VENUS. London, National Gallery (3070).

On wood; 45¾×28 inches (116×71 cm.).

Since the beginning of the eighteenth century, this picture has been held to be an allegory of a season (Spring or Summer) (cf. Baruffaldi, *Vita di C. Tura*, pp. 19, 37). The not very numerous Quattrocento representations of seasons, however, are generally characterized in a clearer and different manner. Gombosi (*Burlington Magazine*, 1933, LXII, p. 71) suggests that the London allegory may represent a sea-goddess (Amphitrite); in his catalogue of Tura's works (1931, p. 15) O. Härtzsch, without giving any specific reason, calls it a 'Venus Metallaria'. That it really is a *Venus* is proved by the small figures in the background: a smith in a cave and a horseman, probably Vulcan and Mars, respectively the husband and lover of the goddess. According to mythological tradition, dolphins, which in this painting adorn the throne, were sacred to Venus. The picture is related to Michele Pannonio's allegory in Budapest (Plate XVI), with which it has in common the motive and composition (a seated, draped divinity), the approximate dimensions (53½×32¼ inches) and the period of execution (first half of the 1460's; Pannonio died about 1464 and left it to Tura to continue the cycle). The Budapest goddess, however, is proved by the attributes and the inscription to be a *Ceres*. Since the rediscovery in 1416 of Manilius's didactic astronomical poem it has been known that the twelve great gods of Olympus were the protecting deities of the Roman months, and as such they were represented a little later in the Schifanoia frescoes, so that it is probable that Tura's *Venus* and Pannonio's *Ceres* are remnants of a cycle consisting of twelve parts, executed immediately before the Schifanoia cycle. In this case Tura's *Venus* would be an allegory of April and Pannonio's *Ceres* one of August (the attribute of a budding cherry twig, which Venus holds in her hand, reminds us of a scene that Duke Borso caused to be added in 1471 to the *May* fresco in Palazzo Schifanoia and which is mentioned by Baruffaldi in his *Vite*, I, p. 72—peasants handing to the duke a basket of early cherries).

The *Venus* has always been attributed to Tura (Baruffaldi, *Vite*, I, p. 80f.). Later scholars have considered the question of its date in conjunction with the problem of its provenance and without any positive reasons have considered both Tura's and Pannonio's allegories to have been part of the pictorial decoration of the villa of Belfiore, which, however, seems highly improbable (see Chronological List of Works, No. 9). As we are unable to say with certainty what was the original destination of the two allegories, the dating of them cannot be based on the known dates of Tura's activity at Belfiore— 1459–63. Even the latter date seems too early for the *Venus*, which, to judge by the degree of stylistic development, is close to the organ door of 1468–9. If Tura continued a cycle of paintings the execution of which had been interrupted by Pannonio's death, then the date of the *Venus* would be about 1465.

Both paintings in all probability formed part of the series of 'four seasons' which about 1540 hung in a small room in front of the Archives of the Palace of the Inquisition near San Domenico in Ferrara (Baruffaldi, *Vita di C. Tura*, pp. 19, 37). In the nineteenth century the *Venus* was in the Costabili collection at Ferrara (C. Laderchi, *Quadreria Costabili*, Ferrara, 1838, I, p. 28; cf. also Padovani, *Critica*, 1954, p. 147 and p. 151); after 1866 it was in the Layard collection, Venice, and since 1916 it has been in London (cf. M. Davies, *National Gallery Catalogue*, 1951, p. 404).

16. PORTRAIT OF A MAN. Washington, National Gallery of Art (Samuel H. Kress collection; 450).

On wood; 14⅛×10⅝ inches (36×27 cm.).

Recognized by A. Venturi (*L'Arte*, 1930, p. 283f.) as a work of Tura's. R. Longhi, on the other hand, attributes it to Marco Zoppo (*Officina Ferrarese*, Rome, 1934, p. 40; C. L. Ragghianti in *Critica d'Arte*, February 1936, is also of this opinion). The uncertainty is probably due to the bad state of preservation of the picture. If, however, we disregard certain details, such as the far too hard outlines —especially of the eyes, nose and headdress—there remains a typical Tura dating from about the same time as the London *Venus* (see Plates 14 and 15). The angular style of the folds is often found in Tura's works, but never in this form in those of Zoppo.

Date: about 1465. The picture was purchased in 1931 by Lord Duveen from the Matthiessen gallery in Berlin; thence it passed to the Kress collection and subsequently to the National Gallery.

17–27. ORGAN-DOOR OF FERRARA CATHEDRAL. Ferrara, Museo del Cattedrale.

Outside: *St. George and the Dragon*.

Inside: *The Annunciation* (on the walls, representations of the seven planets).

On canvas; each side, 162½ × 132 inches (413 × 338 cm.).

On 11 June 1469 Tura was credited with the price of the finished work, which, in view of its large size and careful execution, must have been begun in 1468 (cf. L. N. Cittadella, *Notizie relative a Ferrara*, 1868, I, p. 66). Vasari mentions the work in the 1550 edition of his *Vite* (I, p. 428).

In 1735 the organ was renovated and the paintings were restored by G. B. Cozza (Cittadella, *op. cit.*, p. 67); they were perhaps disfigured by over-painting (see especially the town on the wing, Plate 17) and were then placed in the choir of the cathedral. In 1929 they were removed to their present location and were thoroughly restored in 1947 by A. Raffaldini (cf. Sorrentino-Gnudi, 'Restauro delle ante d'organo', in *Bollettino d'Arte*, 1948, XXXIII, p. 262 f.).

28–31. ST. MAURELIUS ALTAR-PIECE from San Giorgio fuori le mura, Ferrara.

Two tondi from the altar-piece:

The Condemnation of St. Maurelius. Ferrara, Pinacoteca (8).

On wood; diameter 21 inches (53·5 cm.).

The Execution of St. Maurelius. Ferrara, Pinacoteca (9).

On wood; diameter 21 inches (53·5 cm.).

The identification is based on the statement by Baruffaldi that the *St. Maurelius altar-piece* had 'tanti tondini' on which 'gli atti e il martirio di S. Maurelio' were represented; the main pictures are said to have been 'varie immagini di Santi' (*Vite*, I, p. 77). Cittadella (*Notizie relative a Ferrara*, I, p. 698) believes that the appearance of the centre panel has been preserved in a 1489 reproduction of a woodcut showing Maurelius standing with two kneeling donors (from the *Leggenda de Sancto Maurelio*, Ferrara, 1489, fol. l v; reproduced on p. 181 below).

Despite these points of reference, it is difficult to form a concrete idea of the original form of the altar-piece. The surviving tondi seem too large to have been parts of a predella and the woodcut composition too large to have been the centre panel of three or five main pictures showing figures of saints.

Scalabrini (*Chiese di Ferrara*, 1773, Borghi, p. 29) states that the *St. Maurelius altar-piece* was commissioned by the Roverella family, for whom Tura afterwards painted the altar-piece for the same church shown in Plates 52–9. The *St. Maurelius altar-piece* stood in the chapel of the same name on the north side of the choir (cf. A. Superbi, *Apparato*, 1620, p. 122), in which the bones of the saint rest in a fifteenth-century sarcophagus.

In the eighteenth century the surviving tondi were placed in the sacristy (Barotti, *Pitt. e Scult.*, 1770, p. 200; Scalabrini, see above); they then came into the possession of Filippo Zafferini, who bequeathed them in 1817 to the city of Ferrara. In 1836 they were removed to the picture-gallery in the 'Ateneo'.

The dating of the tondi, for which there are no positive points of reference, varies between 'about 1470' (Venturi, *Storia dell'Arte*, 1914, VII, III, p. 530 f.) and 'after 1480' (Ortolani, *Tura, Cossa, Roberti*, 1941, p. 71 f.). The former dating is certainly to be preferred; one might in fact be still more exact and say '1470 or thereabouts', for in them there appears for the first time in the course of Tura's development, even though in only a few details, the 'angular' style found in the Schifanoia frescoes of 1469–71, with that predilection for straight horizontal or vertical lines in the folds of the draperies; see especially Plates 30 and 31.

32–3. MADONNA IN A GARDEN (above: The Annunciation). Washington, National Gallery of Art (Samuel H. Kress collection, 827).

On wood; 20⅞ × 14¾ inches (53 × 37·5 cm.).

This picture shows a combination of painting and plastic elements. Parts of the (lost) chief frame cover the upper part of the picture, enclosing the two 'pictures within a picture' of the Angel and the Virgin of the Annunciation. In the M-shaped ornament which they form, Ortolani (*Tura, Cossa, Roberti*, 1941, p. 21) claims to recognize a 'root of Jesse'. A similar device can be seen on the sarcophagus of the *Pietà* in Vienna (Plate 81; cf. Plate 53 and note to Plates 47–8).

As a clear example of the 'angular style' this picture must be dated in the immediate neighbourhood of the Schifanoia frescoes of 1469–71, or in any case at the end of the 1460's.

In 1917 it was in the possession of Francis Kleinberger, New York, and subsequently in the Pratt, Duveen and H. Kress collections.

34–43. FRESCOES IN THE HALL OF THE PALAZZO SCHIFANOIA, FERRARA.

34–42. THE MONTH OF SEPTEMBER.

Fresco; 177 × 132 inches (450 × 335 cm.).

43. THE ZODIACAL SIGN FOR AUGUST: VIRGO.

Fresco; size of the pictorial plane it occupies: 39⅜ × 44⅛ inches (100 × 112 cm.).

Contents of the *Month of September*: above, Triumph of Vulcan; left, Vulcan's Forge; right, he commits adultery with Venus. On the left of the triumphal car, the Roman she-wolf with Romulus and Remus; on the right, Meteor and Amoretti.

Centre (from left to right): 19th, 20th and 21st decans (ancient astral spirits derived from oriental tradition, each of whom presided over a period of ten days); beneath the 20th decan there is also the zodiacal sign of the Balance, held by a hand.

Below: Duke Borso negotiating with the Venetian ambassador (left); Borso with his courtiers riding out to the chase; in the middle distance at the top, a vintage scene.

Contents of Plate 43: the 17th decan above the zodiacal sign of Virgo (cf. A. Warburg, *Italienische Kunst und internationale Astrologie im Palazzo Schifanoia*, lecture, printed in Rome in 1922, and W. Gundel, *Dekane und Dekansternbilder*, Warburg-Schriftenreihe, Glückstadt-Hamburg, 1936). On the special significance of the Schifanoia frescoes of the months, see above, p. 30f.

All the frescoes in the 'Hall of the Months' were originally attributed to Cosimo Tura (Baruffaldi, *Vita di C. Tura* (about 1706, published in 1836), p. 15f., and *Vite*, I, published 1844, p. 68f.). Nineteenth-century writers, who took a narrower view of the conception of authenticity, rightly considered Tura to be only the leading master in the painting of the hall, who himself executed with his own hand only certain portions. In 1885 Venturi still held to this opinion, but in 1888 he rejected the idea of a personal participation of Tura (*Arte nel periodo di Borso*, in *Riv. stor. ital.*, 1885, II, IV, p. 689f.; *Jahrbuch der preussischen Kunstsammlungen*, 1888, p. 12). R. Longhi (*Officina Ferrarese*, Rome, 1934, pp. 58f., 62, 64f., 72, 75) attributed the *September* to the youthful Ercole Roberti.

In actual fact, five stylistic groups can be clearly distinguished in the Schifanoia frescoes and with regard to two of these we have documentary evidence, according to which Francesco del Cossa painted the east wall of the hall in 1469–70 (Venturi, in *Der Kunstfreund*, IX, 1 May 1885), while Baldassare d'Este altered and completed parts of the work in 1471 (document dated 15 September 1473 in Venturi, *Periodo di Borso*, 1885, p. 721f.). On the basis of stylistic comparison, the painter of the chief portion of the north wall can be clearly identified as Antonio Cicognara (cf. E. Ruhmer, *Zeitschrift für Kunstgeschichte*, 1957, I, p. 94f.). The frescoes on the west wall and portions of those on the south and east walls cannot, for a number of reasons, have been given their definite form until after 1472. There remains the stylistic group to which the *September* belongs, equal, if not superior, in quality to Cossa's frescoes on the east wall. The individual examples of this style are scattered over two walls and provide a model for each type of picture executed in the hall, a model which the other painters can be proved to have followed, for which reason they can be held to be works of the *leading* master. These portions are: (a) the *September*; (b) the 'loggia scene' of *July*; (c) the Virgo in the middle row of the *August*; (d) an intermediate picture at the eastern end of the south wall (group of horsemen). All these portions can be shown with certainty to be the work of Tura himself (for series of comparisons, see E. Ruhmer, loc. cit., pp. 92–3). Cosimo Tura was the leading master in the painting of the hall of the months and executed the portions mentioned to a large extent with his own hand (for further confirmation of this statement, see above, p. 28f.).

On 25 March 1470 the Cossa frescoes and most of the other parts had been completed; in 1471 certain alterations were ordered and additions made, in the execution of which Antonio Cicognara and Baldassare d'Este had a share. The models executed by the leading master must logically have been made as soon as the work began and can therefore be dated about 1469.

In the eighteenth century all the frescoes were covered with whitewash; the work of freeing them began in 1836 and was completed by 1840. The paintings on the west and south walls were almost completely destroyed at that date, if not before; the Tura frescoes are all in a bad state of preservation, with many gaps. They were restored in 1898 and again in 1952–4 by A. Raffaldini.

It is impossible to mention here all that has been written on the frescoes in Palazzo Schifanoia. We will therefore refer the reader to two recent publications containing the most important bibliographical references: G. Bargellesi, *Palazzo Schifanoia*, Bergamo, 1945, p. 20, and C. Padovani, *La Critica d'Arte e la Pittura Ferrarese*, Rovigo, 1954, pp. 195–209 and 483–533.

44. MADONNA WITH SAINTS SEBASTIAN, FRANCIS, DOMINIC AND AGATHA. London, British Museum (256).

Pen-drawing; 5⅞ × 8⅛ inches (14·9 × 21·5 cm.).

On the wainscoting at the back, the word 'horo' (gold), repeated in each compartment. Sketch for an unknown altar-piece. The figure of St. Dominic is used again, slightly modified, in the late fragment of a *St. Dominic* in Florence (Plate 77); the St. Francis of the drawing is akin to Tura's painting of *St. Francis* in Washington (Plate 66). Stylistically, however, the drawing is too remote from the paintings to justify its being considered as a sketch for either the *St. Dominic* or the *St. Francis*. In construction and decoration the throne of the Madonna combines elements from the throne of the London *Venus* (the dolphins; Plate 14) and the throne of the *Madonna* in the *Roverella altar-piece* now in London (the shells of the crown, Plate 53). There is also a stylistic relationship to the *Roverella altar-piece* and the drawing may therefore be dated from the first half of the 1470's. It should be mentioned here that at the end of the eighteenth century C. Cittadella saw 'una picciola Madonna in trono, ed alcuni Santi sul piano' by Tura in the monastery of Sant'Agostino at Ferrara (*Cat. Ist.*, II, p. 211).

Provenance: Collections of J. Richardson, senr., and A. Grahl (cf. Parker, *North Italian Drawings*, London, 1927, p. 26; Popham-Pouncey, *Italian Drawings in the British Museum*, London, 1950, catalogue, p. 158; further bibliography will also be found in this work).

45. ST. JOHN ON PATMOS. Genoa, G. B. Gnecco collection.

On wood; 10⅝ × 12⅝ inches (27 × 32 cm.).

At the 1933 exhibition of Ferrarese painting in Ferrara, was described as 'Ferrarese, affine al Tura' (*Catalogue*, 1933, No. 70 bis, p. 65). R. Longhi (*Officina Ferrarese*, Rome, 1934, p. 39 f.) recognizes it as an authentic work by Tura. The middle portion of the figure has been spoilt by restoration. The painting was probably one of the panels of a predella.

Stylistically it is akin to the drawing shown on Plate 44 and to the *Crucified Christ* of Plate 49, the tapestries (Plates IIc, IIIc) and the drawing of a *Father of the Church* in Bayonne (Plate Xc). It should therefore be dated from the first half of the 1470's.

46. PIETÀ. Formerly Florence, E. Ventura collection.

Painted terracotta; height 21⅝ inches (55 cm.); base 15 × 8⅝ inches.

This sculpture appeared at the 1933 exhibition of Ferrarese painting in Ferrara as 'the work of a Ferrarese sculptor of the end of the fifteenth century, under the influence of Tura' (*Catalogue*, 1933, No. 248, p. 205). Van Marle, who described this *Pietà* as a wood-carving, attributed it to Domenico di Paris, but it is not in accord with the latter's style (*Apollo*, 1935, XXI, p. 12 f.). In view of the incompleteness of our present knowledge of Ferrarese sculpture, it can only be said that the *Pietà* stands alone and cannot be assigned to any well-known

sculptor of Ferrara. On the other hand, in the conception, expression, certain forms and quality it has so many points of contact with Tura's paintings that it can be attributed to him. Tura worked as a sculptor, especially at Belriguardo (cf. Chronological List of Works, *No. 32*); probably he also designed his own picture-frames and in the *Madonnas* of Plates I and 32–3, painting and ornamental carving are so inextricably interwoven that both may well be due to Tura.

The dating of the *Pietà* is necessarily uncertain. Stylistically it is as closely related to the somewhat coarse works of the early 1470's as it is to the latest paintings executed about 1484.

47–8. PIETÀ. Venice, Museo Civico Correr (XVII, 9).

On wood; 17¾ × 12¼ inches (45 × 31 cm.).

Ortolani (*Tura, Cossa, Roberti*, Milan, 1941, p. 40 f.) thought that the signs on the sarcophagus wall were Tura's signature. This statement must be treated with caution. A figure similar to that in the right field occurs in the Washington *Madonna* (Plate 32) and in the Vienna *Pietà* (Plate 81), as well as in a *Pietà* in Chicago (Plate VIII, by an imitator of Tura). For purposes of comparison we reproduce them here:

Venice   Chicago   Vienna

If these are really (very unusual) signatures, there would be at least equal justification for reading the signs in the second field from the right as the figures '72'—all the more so since the date 1472 would, for stylistic reasons, be applicable to the Venice *Pietà*.

There are two replicas of this composition: a painting in the Art Institute, Chicago (from the Ryerson collection; cf. Van Marle, *Apollo*, 1935, XXI, p. 12), which is the work of a feeble imitator, and a brush drawing, madder-red heightened with white (11¾ × 10¼ inches) in the collection of Mrs. Margaret H. Drey, London, which in its original form was, in all probability, executed by Tura's own hand (Plates VIII, IX).

So far as I know, this drawing has never been reproduced, but there is a reference to it in the thesis of O. Härtzsch (*Tura-Katalog*, 1931, p. 41 f.), who dismisses it as a copy. The sheet has numerous tears round the edges, has been considerably reduced by cutting, and important portions of the drawing (the head of the

Virgin, the body of the Christ) have been rubbed out. The missing or blurred portions were later completed in brown wash; the outlines of the Virgin's head, the hands, etc., were redrawn, and the nude was executed afresh. The attitude of Christ's head differs from that in the Venice picture; this may have been an arbitrary alteration by the restorer, but it might also have been so in the original version. In other respects, too, there are noticeable variations from the painting, e.g. in the tip of the Virgin's dress below on the left, and the deliberateness of these variations produces an effect of authenticity. Particularly charming, and characteristic of Tura, is the linear hatching of the calligraphy in the unaltered portions of the Virgin's mantle. Light and shadow are treated with great sureness and nowhere are those misunderstandings discernible which one would expect to find in the work of a copyist.

This drawing is most certainly not a preliminary sketch for the Venice picture; the draughtsmanship is so firm that one can only assume that the painting must have already existed; even this, however, is not a sufficient reason for excluding the London drawing—despite all the disfigurement—from the small group of surviving drawings by Tura.

49. CHRIST ON THE CROSS WITH THE VIRGIN AND ST. JOHN. Cambridge, Fitzwilliam Museum (30–1947).

On wood; 19¾×12 inches (50·2×30·5 cm.).

Perhaps influenced by the *Crucifixion* in bronze (1450–4) by Nicolò and Giovanni Baroncelli and Domenico di Paris in the cathedral at Ferrara. The upper part of the picture has many gaps; it may be doubted whether the view of a town in the background is authentic; the figures look as if they had been damaged by cleaning. Formerly also attributed to Andrea del Castagno.

In its peculiarities of form and the manner in which the folds are arranged, the *Crucifixion* is akin to the works shown in Plates 44, 45, IIc, IIIc, Xc. It must, therefore, have been painted in the first half of the 1470's. From the Tessiers collection it passed to the Cook collection, Richmond, and thence to Cambridge (T. Borenius, *Burlington Magazine*, 1915, XXVII, p. 202).

50–9. THE ROVERELLA ALTAR-PIECE from San Giorgio fuori le mura, Ferrara.

50, 53–6. Centre panel: *The Madonna enthroned with angel musicians* (see frontispiece). London, National Gallery (772).

On wood; 94×40 inches (239×102 cm.).

51. Right wing-panel: *Saints Paul and Maurelius with Nicolò Roverella* (?). Rome, Principe Colonna.

On wood; 60⅝×30 inches (154×76 cm.).

52. Fragment of the left wing-panel: *St. George*. San Diego (California), Fine Arts Gallery.

On wood; 12⅝×11 inches (32×28 cm.).

57–9. Lunette: *Lamentation*. Paris, Louvre (1556).

On wood; 52×105 inches (132×267 cm.).

On the pillars of the Madonna's throne are the tablets of the Hebrew law with the Estensian emblem of fire (see Plates 53–5), which recurs on the top of the throne. Other Estensian emblems are in the right wing-panel (Plate 51): *Steccato* (with lamb) on the bishop's crosier of St. Maurelius and a unicorn in the uppermost cloud. On the top of the throne in the centre panel, the symbols of the four Evangelists; behind the angel the Greek alpha and omega (Plate 53). On the front of the organ-casing in the centre panel, remains of a Latin inscription, which Baruffaldi (*Vite*, I, p. 78) found in 'Lodouico Bigi Pictorii Ferrariensis poetae Tumultuariorum carminum', 1492, the complete inscription reading:

Imago uirginis excitantis filium.
Surge puer. rouorella fores gens pultat. apertum
Redde aditum. pulsa lex ait: intus eris.

According to Baruffaldi's description (*Vite*, I, p. 77f.) the altar-piece was a triptych. Above the two wings, there were two other panels, of the same width but lower, containing figures in half-length. The predella was adorned with scenes from the lives of the Saints, with small figures. A semi-circular lunette formed the top of the altar-piece.

On the left wing, in the foreground stood *St. Peter*, and behind him *St. George*, whose head has been preserved (Plate 52), with a cleric kneeling between them. The centre panel was the painting of the *Madonna* (Plates 50, 53–6). On the right was the surviving wing-panel (Plate 51). In the smaller panels above the wings were half-length figures of *St. Bernard* and *St. Benedict* as bishops, which have been lost. In the predella, which has likewise been lost, were scenes from the legends of these two Saints. The subject of the lunette was the *Lamentation*.

The exact identification of the two kneeling clerics on the wings presents difficulties. According to the chroniclers, one of them was Lorenzo Roverella, bishop of Ferrara after 1460, who died at Monteoliveto between March and July 1474. Baruffaldi states that he was shown knocking on a door, as described in the inscription on the organ mentioned above. Since the kneeling man on the surviving wing is not making this gesture and since he has only a vague family resemblance to the portrait on the tomb of Lorenzo Roverella in San Giorgio (1475; by Ambrogio da Milano), the bishop must have been represented on the lost left wing. The kneeling figure on the right wing is probably his brother Nicolò Roverella, who was prior of the Olivetan convent attached to the church of San Giorgio and died in 1480. (See G. Gruyer, 'La Sculpture à Ferrare', *Gazette des Beaux-Arts*, 1891, extract p. 24; M. Davies, *Catalogue of the National Gallery*, London, 1951, pp. 399–401.)

Since the inscription on the organ speaks of Lorenzo Roverella as a dying man or one just dead, the date of the Roverella altar-piece must have been 1474.

The original location of the altar-piece is described by A. Superbi (*Apparato de gli Hvomini Illustri*, Ferrara, 1620, p. 122) and M. A. Guarini (*Compendio Historico*, Ferrara, 1621, p. 394) as having been 'presso la torre delle campane'; it would therefore seem that the triptych hung above the last altar in the north side-aisle.

According to Baruffaldi (*Vite*, I, p. 80) the Roverella altar-piece was badly damaged during the military operations of 1709. It was taken to pieces and the various parts were dispersed (Boschini, in Baruffaldi, *Vite*, I, p. 80, note). Some of the parts seem to have still been in the sacristy of San Giorgio in 1773 (G. Scalabrini, *Borghi*, p. 29). In any case, in 1787 the *Lamentation* was still in San Giorgio (Frizzi, *Guida di Ferrara*). Together with the *Madonna* it passed to the Zafferini collection (1817). In 1819 the *Lamentation* was in the hands of the dealers Rosini and Fiorani at Brescia; in 1836 it was in the Campana collection, Rome, whence it was taken to France in 1861; in 1863 it was in the Louvre (Perdrizet-Jean, *La Galerie Campana*, Bordeaux, 1907, p. 31; G. de Ricci, Louvre catalogue, 1913, I, p. 149f.).

The *Madonna* passed from the Zafferini to the Frizzoni collection, Bergamo, and in 1867 came into the possession of Charles Eastlake. At the end of the eighteenth century the right wing was in the possession of the vicar of San Tommaso, Ferrara. It then went to the Nagliati collection at Pontelagoscuro near Ferrara and in 1836 to the Colonna collection, Rome. Petrucci gives the same provenance for the two half-length figures of Saints, which, like the predella panels, have since been lost.

The fate of the dismembered left wing is shrouded in obscurity. In 1782 C. Cittadella mentions a 'pezzo' (fragment?) of a *St. George* by Tura in the Rizzoni collection, Ferrara (*Cat. Ist.*, II, p. 212). On the other hand, parts of a large picture by Tura showing half-figures of a St. George and another Saint ('Maurelius') are said to have been in the Costabili collection, Ferrara, with the cut-out half-figure of Christ bearing the Cross on the backs; in 1885 these fragments were sold in Milan (Laderchi, *Quadreria Costabili*, Ferrara, 1838, p. 28, Nos. 25 and 26). In the catalogue of the sale (Sambon, 1885, No. 33), it is even stated that one of the fragments was signed by Tura. The *Head of St. George* now in San Diego was purchased in 1929 from the Lanna collection, Prague. (Bibliography: R. Longhi, *Ampliamenti*, 1940, p. 3f.; O. Härtzsch, *Tura, Pantheon*, 1940, p. 153f.; H. Tietze, 'The St. George by Cosmé Tura', in *The Art Quarterly*, Detroit, 1944, p. 65f.)

With the exception of this head of St. George, of which the hair has been completely repainted, all the surviving portions of the Roverella altar-piece are in a good state of preservation. Longhi (*Officina Ferrarese*, 1934, p. 36) thinks that the three tondi of Plates 60–3 are parts of the predella, but their subject-matter does not correspond with Baruffaldi's description.

60–3. THREE TONDI FROM AN ALTAR-PIECE.

60–1. *The Circumcision*. Boston (Mass.), Isabella Stewart Gardner Museum.

On wood; 15⅜ × 14⅞ inches (39 × 38 cm.).

62. *The Adoration of the Magi*. Cambridge (Mass.), Fogg Art Museum (37).

On wood; 15¼ × 15⅛ inches (38·8 × 38·6 cm.).

63. *The Flight into Egypt*. New York, Metropolitan Museum (Bache) (14.41.49).

On wood; 14⅞ × 14½ inches (38 × 37 cm.).

Said by R. Longhi (*Officina Ferrarese*, Rome, 1934, p. 36f.) to be parts of the Roverella altar-piece. This is, however, doubtful, since Baruffaldi (*Vite*, I, p. 79) states that the predella panels of the Roverella altar-piece contained scenes from the lives of Saints Bernard and Benedict. Stylistically the three tondi are extremely close to the Roverella panels, but the manner is not so highly developed as in the latter and is more closely related to that of the slightly earlier works reproduced on Plates 44, 45 and 49. The tondi must in any case have been painted during the first half of the 1470's.

The *Adoration* and the *Circumcision* came from the Principe Santacroce collection, Rome. The *Adoration* then came into the possession of Principessa Santa Fiora, Rome (Breda, *Rassegna d'Arte*, 1909, p. 170; Benson, *Catalogue of Italian Paintings*, London, 1914, p. 105) and the *Circumcision* into that of Marchesa Passeri, Rome. In the 1880's the *Flight into Egypt* was in the Graham collection, London; subsequently it passed to the Benson collection, London (Venturi, 'L'Arte emiliana', *Arch. Stor. dell'Arte*, 1894, p. 89f.) and later to Lord Duveen.

The colours of the badly preserved *Circumcision* have become so thin owing to cleaning that the drawing is visible, as is the case with the *Crucifixion* of Plate 49.

64-7. DUKE ERCOLE I's PRIVATE ALTAR-PIECE (?). Washington, National Gallery of Art (1089).

Four panels: *St. Francis, Annunciation, St. Maurelius.*

On wood; each 12⅛×4½ inches (30·7×11·5 cm.).

According to Ortolani (*Tura, Cossa, Roberti,* 1941, p. 70f.), these panels formed part of the small altar-piece which the wood-carver Bernardino da Venezia presented to Duke Ercole in 1475. Amadio da Milano was commissioned to add four plates of gilded copper with decorations in niello. On the inside, Tura painted the four figures of Saints on the wings, the *Madonna* on the centrepiece with the Child in her arms. On the outside he first painted four crests of Duke Ercole, who, however, had these removed and replaced by four other Saints. Payments were made to Tura on 27 August and 15 November (the latter for the execution of 'certorum operum sive laborerium'; cf. A. Venturi, *Preussisches Jahrbuch,* 1888, p. 24f.).

Stylistically, 1475 seems a possible date for these little panels. Their artistic tendency points to their having been painted after the Roverella altar-piece of 1474 and has affinities with later works; cf. Plates 71 and 76, and especially 78-9. Venturi assigns the panels to the Roverella altar-piece (*Storia dell'Arte,* 1914, VII, III, p. 532f.). The two figures of Saints recur with certain modifications on several occasions in Tura's works; cf. Plates 10, 44, 76, and also 79 and 83. The figure of St. Maurelius has also points of resemblance to Giovanni Baroncelli's statue of this saint in the bronze *Crucifixion* in Ferrara Cathedral (1450-4).

Provenance: Cook collection, Samuel H. Kress collection (T. Borenius, *Catalogue of the Cook collection,* London, 1913, p. 139).

68. CRUCIFIX (fragment, belonging to the St. Jerome). Milan, Brera (1447).

On wood; 8½×6¾ inches (21·5×17 cm.).

69. ST. JEROME IN PENITENCE (fragment). London, National Gallery (773).

On wood; 39¾×22½ inches (101×57 cm.).

The controversy as to whether these two fragments belong together may be said to have been settled by G. Bargellesi (*Cenobio,* 15 May 1928, p. 11f.; idem, *Notizie di opere d'arte ferraresi,* Rovigo, 1955, p. 17f.). According to C. Cittadella (*Cat. Ist.,* IV, 1783, p. 308),

the praying figure on the right in the London fragment is Duke Borso, but it has no resemblance to him and the identification is improbable since the work cannot have been executed until long after Borso's death (1471); in the smoothness of the technique and the manner of the draperies it is akin to the late works (cf. Plates 72, 81, 83) and must therefore be dated about 1480.

According to Petrucci (Baruffaldi, *Vita di C. Tura,* 1836, p. 37, note), the altar-piece came from the Certosa in Ferrara, perhaps from the ancient church of San Cristoforo. In 1783 the St. Jerome was in the Rizzoni collection, in 1838 in the Costabili collection (Laderchi, *Catalogue,* I, p. 27, No. 13), and in 1867 it was in the possession of Charles Eastlake (cf. M. Davies, *National Gallery Catalogue,* 1951, p. 401f.). The little *Crucifix* was in the Barbicinti collection at Ferrara in 1851 (No. 292; Padovani, *La Critica d'Arte,* Rovigo, 1954, p. 157) and then in that of Cav. Guetta, Venice. Since 1903 it has been in the Brera.

70. HERCULES AND THE LION.

Rotterdam, Boymans Museum (J 243).

Brush-drawing, heightened with white; 8¼×5½ inches (21×15·1 cm.).

The signature 'Gosmè' visible at the top on the right is a later addition, nevertheless it undoubtedly makes a correct attribution, for in its technique the sketch reminds us of Tura's late drawing reproduced on Plate 71, and in the subject, of the *St. Christopher* (Plate 72), while stylistically it belongs to the series of late works executed around 1480.

Provenance: Gigoux collection; Wauters collection; sold by auction in Paris on 23 May 1928 (Drouot); until 1940 in the Koenigs collection, Amsterdam.

71. AN EVANGELIST READING. Florence, Uffizi, Gabinetto delle Stampe (2068).

Brush-drawing, heightened with white; 8⅝×6⅛ inches (21·9×15·5 cm.). Cut out and pasted on.

Ortolani (*Tura, Cossa, Roberti,* Milan, 1941, p. 48) believed that this drawing was a study for the figures of Evangelists executed in 1469-72 in the castle chapel at Belriguardo (see Chronological List, *No. 32*). For stylistic reasons this is improbable, since about 1470 Tura's manner, as numerous examples show, was stiffer and simpler (cf. Plates 28-45). In the drawing the play of the folds is roughly sketched in and is akin to that found in paintings dating from about or after 1480 (cf. Plates 69, 75). It is more likely that the study has to do with a later altar-piece, one of the several that Tura executed (San Luca in Borgo?).

72–4. PARTS OF A POLYPTYCH (A); believed to have been in San Luca in Borgo near Ferrara.

72–3. *St. Christopher.* Berlin, Former Staatliche Museen.

On wood; 29⅞×13⅛ inches (76·8×34 cm.).

74. *St. Sebastian.* Berlin, Former Staatliche Museen.

On wood; 29¾×13 inches (75·7×33·1 cm.).

C. Ricci relates these two pictures and Plates 76, 77 and 80 to an altar-piece once in the church of San Luca (*Rassegna d'Arte*, October 1905, p. 145f.), which Baruffaldi (*Vite*, I, p. 76) mentions together with a similar altar-piece in the Ferrarese church of San Romano and attributes to Tura. From Baruffaldi's statement, however, one can only gather that both were five-winged polyptychs with figures of saints against a gold ground. A third altar-piece, allegedly by Tura, of similar composition was, according to C. Cittadella (*Cat. Ist.*, I, p. 55) in the church of San Giacomo in Argenta (though Ricci, see above, doubts this). From these statements it is impossible to determine which of these and the following pictures, Plates 75–80, of Saints against a gold ground, of almost the same format, belongs to which of the three altar-pieces mentioned or perhaps to other altar-pieces by Tura. C. Cittadella tells us only that the centre panel of the altar-piece in San Giacomo was a *Madonna*, which is perhaps the *Madonna* now in Bergamo (Plate 80).

If we examine all these pictures of Saints of equal format (Plates 72, 74, 75–80) from the point of view of composition, technique and style, we can form three groups, which are clearly distinguishable and were probably parts of three separate altar-pieces. The two paintings in Berlin represent the first group and differ from the other groups in the obviously smaller proportions of the bodies, in the open, almost coarse brushwork and in the presence of landscape backgrounds, lacking in the panels of the other two groups (though this might be due to iconographic requirements).

Despite the stylistic nuances, however, the two Berlin pictures and the other panels of Saints here mentioned have a certain uniformity of style when compared with the next work by Tura of which the date is certain, the *St. Anthony* in Modena (Plates 83–5), painted in 1484. They must therefore have been executed round about 1484. This assumption is supported by two dates known to us which may refer to two of the polyptychs we are discussing. Baruffaldi (*Vite*, I, p. 76) claims to have found in the church archives a document giving the date of 1434 for the execution of the San Luca altar-piece. If the altar-piece is by Tura, then Baruffaldi must have misread the date 1484 as 1434. In the same year 1484, according to

his own statement, Tura painted a smaller 'Sancto Antonio da Padua et certe altre Cosse' (Venturi, *Preussisches Jahrbuch*, 1888, p. 31), which might be identical with the pictures reproduced on Plates 75–7.

Both the Berlin pictures were acquired in 1821 from the Edward Solly collection.

75–7. PARTS OF A POLYPTYCH (B).

75. *St. James Major.* Caen, Hôtel de Ville, Musée des Beaux-Arts (510 (523)).

On wood; 29⅛×12¼ inches (74×31·3 cm.) without the later addition.

76. *St. Anthony of Padua.* Paris, Louvre (1557).

On wood; 28¼×12⅛ inches (72×31 cm.) without the addition.

77. *St. Dominic.* Florence, Uffizi (3273).

On wood; 20×12½ inches (51×32 cm.) without the addition. This panel is a fragment; at the bottom about eight inches have been cut away.

That these three panels originally formed part of one picture is supported first of all by the fact that they are enclosed in decorative frame-paintings which must be the work of an unknown mannerist of the late sixteenth century. The two Saints of Plates 76 and 77 have similar haloes, loosely inserted in the gold ground. All three panels agree in the subtle smoothness of the painting; the delicate, calligraphically regular hatching of the shaded portions and the abstract ornamental quality of the folds. Ortolani (*Tura, Cossa, Roberti*, 1941, p. 62) identified the group of pictures to which he assigned the *St. James* with the altar-piece from San Giacomo, Argenta, on account of the identity of the name of the chief Saint. As, however, the seated *St. James* must have been a centre panel, it cannot have belonged to the San Giacomo altar-piece, which, according to C. Cittadella (*Cat. Ist.*, I, p. 55) had a *Madonna* as its centre panel. In the case of Polyptych B, too, it must remain an open question whether it came from San Luca in Borgo, San Romano or some other church (cf. the notes on Plates 72–4). Nevertheless, it may be assumed that this polyptych also was painted about 1484. The *St. Anthony* of Plate 76 gives the impression of being the immediate predecessor of the 1484 *St. Anthony* of Plate 83, and in that year Tura painted not only a large *St. Anthony*, but also a smaller one together with 'certain other things' —the latter for Bishop Costabili—as he states in a letter he wrote on 9 January 1490 (Venturi, *Preussisches Jahrbuch*, 1888, p. 31). That he mentions, not the centre panel, but one of the wings, might be explained in several ways: the name 'Antonio' might refer to both the large and the small pictures (he says 'similmente'), or else, of the panels for a polyptych, only the *St. Anthony* 'and other trifles' had not been paid for by Bishop Costabili.

The *St. James* panel was formerly in the collection of Cardinal Fesch; it was sold in Rome in 1841, passed to the Mancel collection and in 1872 became the property of the city of Caen (*Catalogue De Giotto à Bellini*, Paris, 1956, p. 90, and *Revue des Arts*, 1956, II, p. 79f. (M. Laclotte)).

The *St. Anthony* in the Louvre formed part of the Campana collection, passed to the Musée Napoléon III in 1862 and since 1863 has been in the Louvre (Perdrizet-Jean, *Collection Campana*, 1907, p. 3, and De Ricci, Louvre catalogue, 1913, I, p. 149f.).

The *St. Dominic* in the Uffizi was acquired in 1906 from an intermediate owner who purchased it from the Canonici collection, Ferrara (Padovani, *Critica d'Arte e Pittura ferrarese*, Rovigo, 1954, p. 136).

78–82. PARTS OF A POLYPTYCH (C); perhaps the altar-piece of San Giacomo, Argenta.

78. *St. Louis of Toulouse* (?). New York, Metropolitan Museum (30.95.259).

On wood; 28½×15⅝ inches (72·4×39·7 cm.).

79. *St. Nicholas of Bari*. Nantes, Musée Municipal des Beaux-Arts (177).

On wood; 29⅛×14⅜ inches (74×36·6 cm.).

80. *Madonna with the Christ Child blessing* (centre panel). Bergamo, Accademia Carrara (Lochis 263).

On wood; 17¾×11¾ inches (45×30 cm.) (cut).

81–2. *The dead Christ supported by two Angels* (lunette). Vienna, Kunsthistorisches Museum (Cat. No. 90; Inv. No. 1867).

Painted on wood, transferred to canvas; 17½×34 inches (44·5×86·7 cm.) (cut).

These four panels have in common the fact that the figures are seen slightly from below, the smoothness of the painting, the hardness of the modelling, the sharpness of the colouring and especially the curving, flowing manner; they are in fact so similar that they may be presumed to have been parts of one and the same altar-piece. As the centre panel is a *Madonna*, one might assume that this was the altar-piece in San Giacomo, which we know had such a centre panel (C. Cittadella, *Cat. Ist.*, I, p. 55).

In all their peculiarities of technique, style and expression, the four panels are extremely close to the *St. Anthony* of Plates 83–5, which is known to have been painted in 1484.

Owing to the large number of *Madonnas* by Tura which eighteenth-century writers believed they had identified, it is useless to try to trace the history of that of Plate 80. In Baruffaldi's time a smaller *St. Nicholas of Bari* by Tura was in the parlour of the monastery of Santa Monica in Ferrara (confirmed by C. Cittadella, *Cat. Ist.*, II, p. 211). The *St. Nicholas* now in Nantes was acquired in 1810 from the Cacault Collection (*Catalogue De Giotto à Bellini*, Paris, 1956, p. 89f.).

The *St. Louis* in New York was identified by Bernard Berenson (1932, p. 591) as by Tura; Ortolani (*Tura, Cossa, Roberti*, 1941, p. 80) doubted whether it was authentic. The picture has, in fact, weak portions (the head, crozier, etc.), which can, however, be explained as due to bad preservation. (H. B. Wehle, *Catalogue of the Metropolitan Museum*, 1941, p. 131.)

The *Pietà* came from the Barbicini collection at Ferrara and was sold in 1846; in 1857 it was acquired by the Vienna Museum from the Adamovics collection. Previously it was attributed either to Marco Zoppo or to Lorenzo Costa (C. Padovani, *Critica d'Arte e Pittura Ferrarese*, Rovigo, 1954, p. 155f.; cf. also von Harck, *Preussisches Jahrbuch*, 1888, p. 36). The composition is found again in a painted and two plastic parallels—the Squarcionesque fresco in the Pellegrini chapel in Sant' Anastasia at Verona and Donatellesque reliefs in Berlin (2439) and in Faenza (Pinacoteca). Of all three variants, Tura's is the latest. On the symbols on the sarcophagus, see note to Plates 47–8.

83–5. ALTAR-PIECE FROM SAN NICOLÒ, FERRARA. Modena, Galleria Estense (9).

St. Anthony of Padua.

On wood; 70⅛×31½ inches (178×80 cm.).

In a letter he wrote on 9 January 1490 (*Preussisches Jahrbuch*, 1888, p. 29f.), Tura states that six years before, i.e. in 1484, he had been commissioned by the chamberlain Francesco Nasello to paint an 'anchona da altaro' for the church of San Nicolò in Ferrara. Baruffaldi (*Vite*, I, p. 64) and C. Cittadella (*Cat. Ist.*, I, 1782, p. 51) saw this *St. Anthony* in that church. Tura does not actually specify the subject of the altar-piece for San Nicolò, but says that 'similmente' he also painted a small *St. Anthony of Padua*, from which one might conclude that the larger picture also represented this Saint. Baruffaldi speaks of a 'tavola del s. Antonio di Padova esposta tuttavia al suo altare nella chiesa parrocchiale di San Nicolò', but by the end of the eighteenth century the Saint had been re-christened San Giacomo della Marca (canonized in 1624). There is, however, no doubt that the Modena picture is a *St. Anthony of Padua* and that it is the altar-piece painted by Tura in 1484 for the church of San Nicolò.

About 1800 the painting passed to the Sacchetti collection; in 1838 it was in the Costabili collection and later, until 1902, in the Santini collection (all in Ferrara; Padovani, *Critica d'Arte e Pittura Ferrarese*, Rovigo, 1954, p. 161f.); it then came into the hands of the dealer Tavazzi and in 1906 was acquired by the Galleria Estense.

The altar-piece was originally larger and, according to C. Cittadella (*Cat. Ist.*, I, p. 51), had a remarkable architectonic frame, of which only a narrow strip still survives. In 1932 it was restored by A. Pellicioli (Pallucchini, *Catalogo della Galleria Estense*, 1952, p. 84).

Woodcut from *Leggenda de Sancto Maurelio*, Ferrara, 1489.
(See the note on the Maurelius altar-piece, p. 173)

MONOGRAPHS ON TURA

This list includes only works with some pretensions to completeness, and also catalogues of Tura's works.

1702–53 Girolamo Baruffaldi
  Vite de' Pittori e Scultori Ferraresi, Ferrara,
  1844–6, I, p. 63 f. Notes by G. Boschini. The
  Vita di Cosimo Tura, written about 1710,
  forms part of this work, but was printed
  separately at Bologna in 1836, with notes by
  G. Petrucci.

1782–3 Cesare Cittadella
  Cosimo Tura in *Catalogo Istorico de' Pittori e
  Scultori Ferraresi*, I, 1782, p. 47 f.

1866 Luigi N. Cittadella
  *Ricordi e Documenti intorno alla vita di
  Cosimo Tura*, Ferrara, 1866.

1888 Adolfo Venturi
  Cosma Tura genannt Cosmè in *Jahrbuch der
  Preussischen Kunstsammlungen*, 9, 1888, p. 3 f.

  Adolfo Venturi
  Cosimo Tura, in *Enciclopedia Italiana*, Vol.
  34, p. 498f. (1937).

1888 Fritz von Harck
  Verzeichnis der Werke des Cosma Tura, in
  Jahrbuch der Preussischen Kunstsammlungen,
  1888, p. 34f.

1892 Gustave Gruyer
  Cosimo Tura, in *L'Arte*,
  October–November 1892, p. 1 f.

1907 Bernard Berenson
  Tura, in *North Italian Painters of the Renaissance*, New York–London (catalogue, p.
  297f.).

1931 Otto Härtzsch
  *Katalog der echten und fälschlich zugeschrie-
  benen Werke des Cosimo Tura*. Thesis, Hamburg, 1931 (polygraph reproduction of
  portion of a manuscript).

1934 Roberto Longhi
  Officina Ferrarese, Rome, 1934, pp. 34f.,
  203 f.

1939 Giorgio Gombosi
  Cosimo Tura, in Thieme-Becker, *Künstlerlexikon*, Vol. 33, p. 480f.

1941 Sergio Ortolani
  *Cosmè Tura—Francesco del Cossa—Ercole
  Roberti*, Milan, 1941.

1951 Benedict Nicolson
  The Painters of Ferrara, London, 1951. With
  a catalogue of Tura's paintings.

1952 Alberto Neppi
  Cosmè Tura, Milan, 1952 (Premio Gastaldi).

INDEX OF PLACES

REPRODUCTIONS OF WORKS BY OTHER MASTERS